BEHIND EVERY GREAT *Tradie*

is a woman rolling her eyes

🐢 TurtlePublishing

Copyright © 2025 Helen Cowley

The information in this book is based on the author's experiences, opinions and research. While every effort has been made to ensure its accuracy at the date of publication/circulation, this material is of a general, educational nature and is guidance only. It should not be interpreted as legal or other specific advice, nor should it be taken as being completely free of error or omission. As this material may not necessarily be a fully comprehensive coverage of any topic nor cover all specific situations. Before acting or relying upon any of the information in this material, you should seek appropriate professional and or legal advice in regards to your specific circumstances.

The author and publisher disclaims responsibility for any adverse consequences, which may result from the use of the information therein.

All rights reserved. No part of this publication may be reproduced, stored in or introduced into a retrieval system, or transmitted in any form, or by any means (electronic, mechanical, photocopying, recording or otherwise) without the prior written permission of the author. Any person who does any unauthorised acts in relation to this publication will be liable to criminal prosecution and civil claims for damages.

First published by Turtle Publishing 2025

Cover & Illustrations by Turtle Publishing

turtlepublishing.com.au

Contents

About the Author   ix
Thankyou   xi
Introduction   xvii

Chapter 1 1
'I'm Just Helping Out' – Famous Last Words

How It All Began (AKA My biggest mistake)

Welcome to the Engineering Business (Where the fun never ends!)

The Unspoken Rule: If you can use a computer, you're now the boss

The First Time I Rolled My Eyes and Knew It Was Over

How Passion Creeps Up on You

Lessons Learned

Chapter 2 13
The Million-Dollar Idea (That will cost us a fortune)

The Spark of Genius (AKA The beginning of my headache)

The Classic Tradie Business Plan

The Time Andrew almost built another Widget (Without a plan)

The Best Tradie Ideas Always come in the Middle of Other Jobs

The Rare Unicorn: A Tradie who actually finishes the Idea

Lessons Learned

Chapter 3 23
'*Hon*, Just Write THE Business Plan for My Genius Invention'
From 'Quick Business Plan' to a Lifetime Commitment

The First Business Plan: A Masterpiece of Optimism

Learning Marketing the Hard Way (Without social media!)

His Idea, My Life – The Reality of Supporting a Visionary

Lessons Learned

Chapter 4 33
'We Need 10 Staff for This Job. Yesterday.'
Hiring Tradies: The Ultimate Crash Course

The Interview Process: Separating the Talkers from the Doers

The Chinook Helicopter Enthusiast: A Cautionary Tale

Inductions, Training & Trying to Keep Some Control

The Reality of Managing a Growing Team

Lessons Learned

Chapter 5 43
The Great Divide: Tools vs. Paperwork
'You Do the Paperwork, I'll Do the Work That Matters'

How 'Helping Out' Turned into a Full-Time Office Job

The Art of Looking Calm While Internally Screaming

When You Handle the Admin, You Hold the Power

Setting Boundaries: The Key to Survival

Lessons Learned

Chapter 6 53
'You Can't Read Plans, But You Can Manage the Project!'
She doesn't read plans—but she knows the schedule, the staff, and the budget

The Unwritten Rule: 'Just Wait for Andrew'

The 'Andrew Will Be Back Later' Experiment

When You're 'The Woman Behind the Man'—But Actually Running Everything

Lessons Learned

Chapter 7 63
'Oh My God – Just Do the Job!'
The Great Electrical Debate (or how to make a grown woman cry over amps and voltage)

Ordering Parts: The Left-Handed Screwdriver Special

Lessons Learned

Chapter 8 71
'I'll Just Pop in and Tell You What You Did Wrong'
Welcome to the 'What You Missed' Review

The Time He Argued with the Draftsman (and won?!)

The Art of Pretending to Take Feedback While Planning Revenge

Lessons Learned

Chapter 9 81
'You're Not Fired Until a Man Says So!'
Congratulations, You're Now the Entire HR Department!

Hiring Tradies: A Masterclass in Filtering Out the 'Know-it-Alls'

The Realisation: Just Because They Have a Ticket Doesn't Mean They Know What They're Doing

Why Do My Eyes Roll? Let Me Count the Reasons...

Lessons Learned

Chapter 10 91
'We Don't Really Need Staff Living With Us... Do We?'
How We Became an Unofficial Halfway House

When Your Staff Are Your Drinking Buddies, You've Got a Problem

Why We Needed to Draw the Line (And why it took so long)

Lessons Learned

Chapter 11 99
We Didn't Make a Profit, But We Have All the Excuses
Where Did the Money Go? (Hint: It wasn't profit)

The Great Cash Flow Catastrophe

Reverse Planning: The Financial Trick That Saved My Sanity

How to Handle Clients Who Think 30 Days Means 'Whenever I Feel Like It '

Lawyers Aren't Just for Rich People (or big problems)

The Machinery Widget that 'Was Definitely Necessary'

Lessons Learned

Chapter 12 111
Lockable Gates & Learning to Say No
Where Communication Meets Chaos...

Welcome to the Christmas Day Wake-Up Call From Hell

Lessons Learned

Chapter 13 119
Love Letters and Tracking Calls
Newsletters: AKA Client 'Love Letters'

Lessons Learned

Chapter 14 129
Balancing Babies, Business, and Board Meetings – Welcome to the Ultimate Juggle
The Business-Baby Balancing Act

Training Children Like Future CEOs (Or at least, future quiet humans in an office)

Breastfeeding in the Office – The Cloth Nappy Camouflage

Meetings in the Office: The Best Receptionist in the World

Toolbox Meetings & Feeding Times – A Timing Disaster

Lessons Learned

Chapter 15 139
Beyond the Toolbox – The Skills That Keep the Big Jobs Running

Big Jobs Need More Than Big Tools

The Bigger Picture – Seeing Beyond the Next Job

Growing a Business? Here's What No One Tells You

What I Learned (The hard way) About Running a Growing Business

Burnout Mindset – When the Business Owns You

The Moment I Realised I Was More Than the Business

Leading Into 'Wait… What About Me?'

Lessons Learned

Chapter 16 153
'Wait, What About Me?' – Reclaiming Your Life & Sanity

The Moment I Realised I Had Lost Myself

When Clients Saw My Value Before I Did

The Two Big Lies I Told Myself

Reaching My Breaking Point: The Moment I Chose Myself

The Art of Letting Go: Downsizing a Business the Hard Way

Lessons Learned

Afterword 165
A Woman, A Business, and a Life Worth Living

About the Author

Helen Cowley is a business strategist, author, and founder of **Small Business Improvement Services** (SBIS) and **The Business Workroom**. With over 35 years of experience in business development, leadership, and small business consulting, she specialises in helping family-owned and trades-based businesses create clarity, structure, and sustainable growth.

Through her coaching programs and practical frameworks—including the *SBIS Business Management Wheel of Growth*—Helen supports business owners in developing key capabilities across planning, systems, finance, marketing, and leadership. Her unique approach combines strategic thinking with grounded, real-world insight, making her a sought-after advisor for businesses navigating growth, complexity, or transition.

Helen's work is driven by a mission to empower business owners—particularly those in small, often informal, family-run operations—to step into confident leadership, and develop businesses that are both profitable and personally fulfiling.

A message from Helen...

"*Behind Every Great Tradie Is a Woman Rolling Her Eyes* is my honest, and sometimes hilarious, take on what it really means to run a business from behind the scenes. It shines a light on the resilience, smarts, and humour women bring to the table—often without the title or the credit. My hope is that it reminds you that you're not just surviving this—you have what it takes to build something that truly thrives."

About the Author

Helen Cowley is a business strategist, author, and founder of **Small Business Improvement Services** (SBIS) and **The Business Workroom**. With over 35 years of experience in business development, leadership, and small business consulting, she specialises in helping family-owned and trades-based businesses create clarity, structure, and sustainable growth.

Through her coaching programs and practical frameworks—including the *SBIS Business Management Wheel of Growth*—Helen supports business owners in developing key capabilities across planning, systems, finance, marketing, and leadership. Her unique approach combines strategic thinking with grounded, real-world insight, making her a sought-after advisor for businesses navigating growth, complexity, or transition.

Helen's work is driven by a mission to empower business owners—particularly those in small, often informal, family-run operations—to step into confident leadership, and develop businesses that are both profitable and personally fulfilling.

A message from Helen...

"*Behind Every Great Tradie Is a Woman Rolling Her Eyes* is my honest, and sometimes hilarious, take on what it really means to run a business from behind the scenes. It shines a light on the resilience, smarts, and humour women bring to the table—often without the title or the credit. My hope is that it reminds you that you're not just surviving this—you have what it takes to build something that truly thrives."

Thankyou

To the ones who made this possible

Writing this book has been a journey—a mix of reminiscing times, conversations, laughter, lessons, late-night eye rolls, and the occasional 'why am I even doing this?' moment.

But more than anything, it's been a reflection of the incredible people who shaped my life, my business, and my understanding of what it truly means to build something lasting.

So, before we dive into the chaos, humour, and real talk about running a business and reclaiming yourself, I want to take a moment to say thank you.

To the Tradies
Who dream big (and get distracted even bigger)

To the tradies who wake up one morning with a *million-dollar idea*, get halfway through a job, and then come running into the office with a new 'genius' plan—this book is for you.

- ✓ For the ones who build, fix, and create—without thinking about spreadsheets, contracts, and cash flow (but should).

- ✓ For the ones who have big ambitions but no time to stop and plan them out.

- ✓ For the ones who know their trade inside and out—but are still figuring out the business side.

Your work is valuable. **Your ideas are brilliant.** But behind every great tradie? There needs to be a plan that keeps it all running.

I hope this book gives you a laugh, some insight, and maybe even a few lightbulb moments about how to **grow your business without losing your sanity** *(and/or your wife).*

To the Women
Who 'just help out' but actually run the whole show

To the wives, partners, and silent business managers who were just supposed to help with a little admin but somehow ended up running the finances, organising the projects, managing the staff, and keeping everything from falling apart—this book is especially for you.

✓ For the women who do it all but never take the credit.

✓ For the ones who juggle businesses, babies, budgets, and breakdowns all before lunch.

✓ For the ones who were never 'trained' in business but somehow became the backbone of one.

I see you.

I was you.

And if this book does anything, I hope it helps you recognise your worth, your skills, and your right to build something for yourself on your own terms—whether it's inside or outside the business.

To My Family
Who had no choice but to be part of this ride

To my children, who grew up watching, learning, and sometimes being bribed into sitting quietly while I took business calls, thank you for teaching me patience, resilience, and the true meaning of multitasking. It has been a true joy to have a front row seat to watching you all grow into the adults you are today.

To my husband, Andrew, who allowed me to use our lives in this book. Despite the million ideas, last-minute projects, and occasionally testing my sanity, you have not only been an engineer, builder, and inventor, but also a constant source of support—thank you for always believing in what we could build together. **And what you have encouraged me to do.**

To my sister Alice and brother-in-law Graham, who stretched my ideas, stories and the use of great words, knowing that when you run a business, big or small, there are always times when you have to just roll your eyes and laugh rather than cry.

To the friends, mentors, and clients who have been part of this **wild business journey**, thank you for the lessons, the challenges, and the opportunities to grow.

And Finally—to you, the Reader

Whether you picked up this book for a laugh, for advice, or because you're in the thick of running a business and wondering if you're the only one struggling, thank you for being here.

- ✓ If you're in business, I hope this book gives you clarity, direction, and a few 'oh, that's me' moments.

- ✓ If you're supporting someone else's business, I hope this book helps you see just how much you contribute.

- ✓ And if you're at a crossroads, I hope this book reminds you that your life, your time, and your future are yours to shape.

This book isn't just about tradies, businesses, or burnout—it's about building a life that works for you.

And if you take one thing away from it, let it be this:

You are more capable than you realise. You are already skilled. And you deserve a business (and a life) that doesn't just run well—but makes you happy.

So, let's dive in.

Let's talk about the business, the chaos, the lessons, and the laughter.

And let's roll our eyes at the tradies we love—while quietly making sure everything still runs smoothly.

Because behind every great tradie... there's a woman keeping it all together.

And this book is for you.

Introduction

Welcome to the Wild Ride, Tradie Wives

If you're reading this, chances are you've uttered some version of the following phrase at least once in your life:

'I'm just helping out.'

Ah, *marriage* – the land of *'just helping'*.

Maybe you started by answering a few calls. Maybe you helped send out some invoices. Maybe you just happened to know how to turn on a computer, and suddenly, you were the go-to person for all things admin, finance, HR, and marketing.

And before you knew it, **BOOM**—you were running an entire bloody business without ever actually applying for the job.

The Tradie Wife Initiation
AKA How we all end up here

My story isn't unique.

I, like so many other women, started off thinking *I was just supporting my husband's business.*

I'd already run my own shoe and accessories retail shop for six years. I had:

✓ Managed stock control *(12 months ahead, because retail isn't for the disorganised).*

✓ Controlled cash flow *(because suppliers don't take 'Oops, I forgot' as a payment method).*

✓ Dealt with staff, suppliers, and customers *(some lovely, some utterly unhinged).*

✓ Survived the rolling door of pitchmasters—sales reps and their endless cups of coffee *(which may explain why I'm now allergic to the stuff).*

✓ Bought the shop as a partnership. The husband took one look and bolted for the tool shed. *Turns out, wrangling machinery is easier than wrangling kids' feet into school shoes and ladies into high heels!*

✓ Back to work with a newborn in tow *(because nothing says work-life balance like serving customers while covered in baby spew!)*

✓ Balanced business and mothering of 2 children *(because why not make life even more chaotic?)*

So, when my husband, Andrew, casually asked:

'*Hon*, can you just help out with some admin?'

I thought, *Sure!* A few invoices and phone calls? No problem! Baby number 3 on the way, I've got this!

HUGE. MISTAKE.

Because if you know anything about tradies, you know that they hate admin with a passion.

So once they realise that you can handle it?

Game over.

Suddenly, my 'few invoices' turned into:

- Full-blown bookkeeping and accounts management *(because someone had to do it)*.
- HR and hiring staff *(because 'he's a good bloke' is not a recruitment strategy)*.
- Project management *(because Andrew could build anything, but mustering cats? Forget it)*.
- Customer service and crisis management—aka Andrew's worst nightmare *(because handling 6 am conflict is harder when you'd rather hide in the storeroom)*.
- Inventor's assistant *(because, of course, Andrew wasn't just happy fixing things—he wanted to build new things)*.

- Master of manusha—endless admin, sorting calls, and fixing mistakes I didn't make *(because the likes of Telstra fairy and Origin gremlins work overtime).*

And before I knew it, I wasn't helping anymore.

I was running an engineering business.

And if that wasn't enough?

I was raising four of my five children at the same time.

Oh yes. **FIVE.**

So if you're wondering, 'Does Helen really know what she's talking about?' let me assure you—**I have earned every single eye roll in this book.**

Who Is This Book For?
Hint: If you're reading this, it's probably you

This book is for the **unsung heroes of the tradie world**—the wives, partners, and women who somehow find themselves:

✓ Running a business they didn't mean to sign up for.

✓ Managing a bunch of tradies who act like they don't need rules (until everything goes wrong).

- ✓ Answering calls from clients at ridiculous hours.
- ✓ Spending hours on *Manusha* handling.
- ✓ Negotiating with suppliers who mysteriously change their pricing every other week.
- ✓ Wondering how the hell they got here.

It's for the women who **never planned on running a business** but somehow became the **CEO, CFO, HR Manager, Marketing Director, and Crisis Negotiator**—all while still making dinner. You are the reason I started my own consulting and coaching business.

This book is for you.

What You'll Find in These Pages

This isn't some **boring business manual** filled with complicated jargon and textbook advice.

This is **real talk from a woman who lived it**—who learned the hard way, made the mistakes, figured things out, and now wants to pass those lessons on to you.

Inside, you'll find:

- ✓ Hilarious, painfully relatable stories about life as a tradie wife.

✓ Lessons learned the hard way *(so you don't have to make the same mistakes).*

✓ Practical advice on running the front and back office, managing staff, dealing with difficult clients, and handling cash flow.

✓ Why boundaries matter *(because if you don't set them, you will drown in this business. And may lose yourself in the process.)*

✓ How to reclaim your own identity *(because you are more than just 'the woman behind the business').*

And most importantly...

✓ **You'll laugh.** *A lot.*

Because let's be honest—**if you don't laugh at the madness, you'll cry.**

The Hard Lessons
That no one warns you about

I didn't think I was qualified to do any of this.

Like so many other tradie wives, I thought, *'Who am I to run a business? I don't have a degree. I don't have training.'*

But here's what I've learned:

Experience beats qualifications every time. Qualifications just add - but more about that later.

It turns out that **years of running a business, managing staff, negotiating with suppliers, and dealing with clients is way more valuable** than a fancy business degree.

So if you're doubting yourself—if you're wondering, *'Do I actually know what I'm doing?'*—let me tell you right now:

You do!

You are **stronger, smarter, and more capable than you realise.**

And if I can figure this out while raising five kids and running a fabrication business, so can you.

A Final Word Before We Dive In...

If you're already deep into this tradie-wife life, you'll **recognise yourself in these pages.**

If you're just starting out, **consider this your warning.**

And if you've been in this game for a while but need a **good laugh** and some practical advice, you're in the right place.

Because here's the truth:

- ✓ This life will challenge you.
- ✓ It will test your patience *(and your ability to keep a straight face).*
- ✓ You will roll your eyes at least 100 times a day.
- ✓ And yes, you will probably wonder, *'How the hell did I end up here?'*

But it will also **teach you skills you never thought you'd learn.**

And somewhere along the way, you'll realise...

Behind every great tradie is a woman rolling her eyes... and keeping the whole damn thing together.

Now, let's dive in.

Tradie Talk: *Manusha – If you are a country person, you will understand that sometimes you have to shovel manure from one point to another unnecessarily. In business, 'manusha' defines the waste of time when 'sorting things out'. A waste of time to spend an hour and a half talking and waiting on the phone for someone who has no idea how to fix your problem! Or blames you for changing something you have no authority to change because it has happened in their system or from some software change or someone accidentally flicking a switch. But you have to waste your valuable time – not get paid for it, and it's not your fault. Some weeks I have had at least four such phone calls and wondered why I didn't achieve my plan!!!! But you have spend hours on the phone sorting out manusha.*

Chapter 1

'I'm Just Helping Out' – Famous Last Words

How 'a bit of admin' turned into running a full-blown business (and a lifetime of eye rolling).

Helen Cowley

How It All Began (AKA My biggest mistake)

'*Hon, can you just help out with some admin?*'

That was it.

That **one** innocent question—so casual, so harmless—was the moment my life took a turn I never saw coming.

At the time, I was already an experienced businesswoman—*or so I thought.*

I had run my own shoe and accessories retail shop for six years. But I wasn't just selling pretty things—I was bringing fashion to life, one statement piece at a time. I wasn't just picking stock; I was curating a collection that made people feel stylish, confident, and just a little bit fabulous.

- ✓ Managing stock *(12 months ahead on indent ordering, because retail is a game of predictions, and trends wait for no one).*

- ✓ Controlling cash flow *(because suppliers expect their money, even when customers spend an hour debating nude vs. blush heels).*

- ✓ Dealing with customer service *(which mostly involved listening to 'these shoes gave me blisters' complaints—after they'd danced through an entire wedding).*

✓ Balancing business and motherhood while raising two kids *(because why juggle handbags when you can juggle life instead?)*.

✓ Living and breathing fashion *(from sourcing bold, coloured stockings to pairing the perfect hats, scarves, and statement jewellery—because no outfit is complete without a little extra flair)*.

So, when Andrew asked me to *'just help out with a bit of admin,'* I thought:

'Sure! A few invoices and phone calls? No problem!'

Oh, what a fool I was.

Because, as I quickly learned, *'just helping out'* is tradie-speak for **'Congratulations! You now run an engineering business.'**

Welcome to the Engineering Business (Where the fun never ends!)

Running a retail shop? *Challenging but manageable.*

Running an engineering business full of tradies? *A completely different beast.*

Suddenly, I wasn't just dealing with shoes and handbags.

I was dealing with:

✓ Contracts *(which were about as easy to read as ancient hieroglyphics)*.

✓ Project management *(trying to get tradies to meet deadlines without threatening their lives)*.

✓ Inventing stuff *(because Andrew didn't just want to fix things—he wanted to CREATE things)*.

✓ Negotiating with suppliers *(who somehow always had 'unexpected price increases')*.

✓ Chasing overdue payments *(because some clients thought 'net 30' meant 'pay whenever you feel like it')*.

✓ Wrestling with national contractors *(who delivered the wrong plans, made mistakes, blamed me, then rewrote the rules like they were starring in their own reality show)*.

✓ And don't forget the *Manusha* every business deals with.

And the best part?

Nobody trained me for this.

There was no *Welcome to Running a Tradie Business Handbook* when I started.

I was **thrown in the deep end**, headfirst, and expected to swim.

And if I so much as hesitated, Andrew would flash that **cheeky tradie grin** and say:

"Hon, you're just naturally good at this stuff!'

Translation: 'I don't want to do it, so now it's your problem.'

The Unspoken Rule: If you can use a computer, you're now the boss

Now, here's a **universal truth** about tradie businesses:

If you can turn on a computer, you are now in charge of **EVERYTHING.**

In those days, it was more about my ability with spreadsheets.

Oh, did you think knowing how to type just means sending a few emails?

WRONG.

If you can type, it means you are now responsible for:

✓ Quoting and invoicing *(because 'we'll figure it out later' is NOT an acceptable pricing strategy).*

✓ Payroll *(because tradies don't work for free, even if you sometimes do).*

✓ HR and hiring *(which, let's be honest, is mostly figuring out how NOT to hire blokes who can't show up on time).*

✓ Chasing unpaid invoices. *A delicate dance of 'Hey mate, just following up' and 'PAY UP OR ELSE!'.*

✓ Contracts and compliance *(because reading through 40 pages of legal jargon is definitely what I had planned for my evenings).*

✓ Watching in horror as the cost estimator cheerfully gave away all our hard-earned tradie shortcut cost advantages *(because why keep a competitive edge when you can hand it out for free? And you lose potential tenders).*

And let's not forget...

✓ Inventor's Assistant

Oh yes.

Because Andrew wasn't just happy **running a business.**

No, no.

He wanted to **change the world** and **revolutionise the industry.**

So, in addition to admin, finance, HR, and project management, I was also expected to support his latest invention ideas.

I can't tell you how many times I found myself standing in the workshop, nodding along as Andrew explained a machine he was designing, all while secretly wondering:

'How on earth did I end up here?' rolling my eyes so hard they might get stuck.

The First Time I Rolled My Eyes and Knew It Was Over

Every woman in a tradie business has **that moment.**

The moment when she realises:

'Oh no. This is my life now.'

For me?

It was when **I wrote my first business plan.**

Now, I had never planned to write a business plan.

I thought that's for big business, and that was Andrew's job—he was the one with the big ideas, the passion, the grand vision.

But, as it turns out, tradies are fantastic at dreaming... and terrible at paperwork.

So when Andrew came to me with an idea—something about building a subarc machine for repairing rollers and idlers on earthmoving machinery—and casually mentioned that we might need some funding to get it going, I made a critical mistake.

I asked:

'Have you got a plan – like a business plan?'

He blinked. **Twice, maybe three times.**

Then grinned and said,

'Nah, *Hon*, but you're great at that stuff!'

And just like that, I was up to my elbows - writing a business plan.

How Passion Creeps Up on You

At first, I was just **putting some thoughts together**.

You know, *'helping out'*.

But then something **dangerous** happened. Which I now understand as one of the benefits of business planning.

- ✓ I started researching.
- ✓ I started structuring the plan.
- ✓ I started thinking about how to market it, how to sell it, how to make it profitable.

And the worst part?

I started getting excited.

Because, of course damn it, the idea was actually brilliant.

It made sense.

It had potential.

And before I knew it, I wasn't just writing a business plan—I was creating the passion and planning a future for this product.

By the time I finished, I handed it to Andrew with a strange mix of pride and dread.

'*Hon*, this is amazing!' he said.

And then—before I could stop him—

'So… can you run with this?'

And **that's when I caught myself rolling my eyes for the first time**—a moment of pure clarity that things were only going downhill for me and my role as the wife of a tradie.

Lessons Learned
Business Plans are Dangerous

- ✓ Never ask a tradie if they have a business plan unless you're prepared to write it... if you do, it is your plan, not his!!

- ✓ Writing a plan isn't just about strategy—it's about creating passion.

- ✓ If you make something look too good, congratulations—you're now in charge.

- ✓ Eye-rolling is a survival skill.

- ✓ Passion is great—just be aware it comes with an unpaid job offer.

Final Thought
Beware of Passion—It Comes with a To-Do List

That business plan? It worked.

Andrew built his subarc machine.

We got sourced funding. We landed contracts. We grew the business.

And me?

I had gone from *'just helping with admin'* to writing business plans, working the subarc (*the only welding I can actually do after 45 years*), running projects, planning, marketing, and finance.

So, my advice?

Beware of passion—it comes with a to-do list. And so do business plans.

Behind every great tradie is a woman rolling her eyes... because she accidentally convinced herself to run the business.

Tradie Talk: *Arc In welding, the 'welding arc' is the intense, high-temperature plasma formed by an electric arc between a welding electrode and the workpiece, creating the heat necessary to melt and join metals.*

Chapter 2

The Million-Dollar Idea (That will cost us a fortune)

Because every tradie has that one - sorry - ten ideas that will make millions... and you're the one who has to make it happen.

The Spark of Genius (AKA The beginning of my headache)

Lets go back a step to the previous conversations - **Every tradie has that one idea.**

That brilliant, game-changing, revolutionary invention that is *guaranteed* to make millions.

At least, in their mind.

For Andrew, these lightbulb moments would appear at the most inconvenient times:

- ✓ In the middle of a job, mid-weld, suddenly seeing this would be much easier if.... off into the distance like a mad scientist.

- ✓ At 10 pm, just as I was finally relaxing, only to hear, *'Hon! I just thought of something!'*

- ✓ During important meetings, when he should be listening, he's sketching something *groundbreaking* on the front of a receipt that was needed for tax records.

And so the inevitable conversation would begin:

'*Hon*, I've got it. This is THE ONE. This idea is going to change everything!'

Cue **me nodding supportively** while simultaneously googling *'How to say no to a tradie without crushing his soul.'*

The Classic Tradie Business Plan

A tradie's business plan for these *groundbreaking* ideas usually follows a **predictable pattern:**

1. Think of the idea. *Hon, this is gonna be HUGE.*

2. Start building something immediately. *No time for research—I need to get into the workshop right now!*

3. Spend money on materials, even though the numbers haven't been checked. *We have to spend money to make money, Hon!*

4. Ask me to figure out the paperwork, the marketing, and the sales. *Can you just do the business side of things? You're good at that stuff.*

5. Realise six months later that he's already moved on to the next brilliant idea.

And just like that, the *million-dollar idea* has now become a **very expensive distraction.**

Helen Cowley

The Time Andrew almost built another Widget (Without a plan)

One of my favourite examples of *'the idea that will make us rich'* was Andrew's concept of making things easier and quicker.

It started **innocently enough.**

One day, he came into the office, covered in grease and excitement, and declared:

'Hon, I've figured it out. A fully automated welding system! We're going to be millionaires.'

I looked up from the actual **business paperwork that kept our company running** and sighed.

'That's great, *hon*. What's the plan?'

His response?

'We'll figure it out as we go!'

No.

No, we will not.

Because *'figuring it out as we go'* was the exact reason why we had a workshop full of half-finished projects, spare parts, and machines that started as *'the next big thing'* but ended up as very expensive paperweights.

I took a deep breath and **tried** to be the voice of reason.

'Okay, let's break this down. Have you worked out the costs?'

'Not yet, but it won't be much.'

(That was a lie. It would definitely be much.)

'Have you checked if there's a market for this?'

'Hon, trust me, people will want it.'

(Another lie. People might want it, but not without testing, pricing, and, oh, I don't know, a proper plan!)

I tried **one last time.**

'Can you at least finish the other five projects before starting this one?'

*At this point, he looked genuinely **offended.***

'Hon, this is different. This is THE idea.'

And with that, he walked back to the workshop, muttering about blueprints and welding precision, leaving me to wonder **how many zeros this *'brilliant idea'* was going to add to our expenses.**

Helen Cowley

The Best Tradie Ideas Always come in the Middle of Other Jobs

Here's another **common trait** of tradies with big ideas:

They get **distracted by genius** in the middle of doing something **completely unrelated**.

One time, Andrew was in the middle of a completely normal fabrication job when he suddenly froze, dropped his tools, and ran toward the office.

I panicked.

'Is something wrong?!'

'Hon, listen. What if we designed a portable, self-cleaning welding table?'

Oh. My. God.

'Can you please just finish the job you're working on first?'

'*Hon*, this could be the one that makes us millions!'

'Yes, but if we don't finish this actual paid job, we won't make enough money to pay for dinner!'

This is what **living with an inventor/tradie/business owner hybrid** looks like.

Project Feasibility & Risk

The Rare Unicorn: A Tradie who actually finishes the Idea

Now, don't get me wrong—some tradies actually follow through on their million-dollar ideas.

And to be fair, Andrew wasn't your typical scatterbrained, forgetful tradie when it came to tools or getting the job done.

His truck was always organised—every tool in its place, nothing left behind. If he needed a specific spanner, he knew exactly where it was.

Unlike some tradies who seem to treat their utes like mobile junkyards, Andrew believed that having the right tool at the right time was half the battle.

And when it came to ideas that actually made sense?

Some of them were **brilliant.**

- ✓ He had genuine time-saving innovations that made our jobs easier.
- ✓ He thought outside the box, coming up with solutions to real problems in the industry.
- ✓ Some of his ideas were profitable, and a few of them even saved us thousands in efficiency gains.

But—and this is important—not every idea was a million-dollar winner.

Some, just cost a fortune in parts and late nights in the workshop.

The key difference?

Knowing when to back a great idea... and when to politely suggest he 'finish the last one first.'

Some tradies actually follow through on their million-dollar ideas.

But these ones are rare—like a clean ute interior or a tradie who remembers to bring home the milk for the children instead of just a carton of beer.

When you **do** find one, hold onto him like a winning lottery ticket.

These are the tradies who don't just dream big—they:

✓ Research the market before spending money.

✓ Actually listen when someone suggests a business plan.

✓ Finish what they start before jumping to the next big thing.

And do you know what happens when one of these mythical creatures gets an idea?

They actually turn it into something profitable.

Project Feasibility & Risk

Lessons Learned
How to Handle your Tradie's 'Million-Dollar Idea'

✓ Stay calm *(you've been here before; you will be here again)*.

✓ Ask the real questions. *Have you costed this? Who's the customer? Is it even possible?*

✓ Delay tactics work. *That sounds great! Let's look at it in a month after we finish these other projects.*

✓ Never let them spend money before Step 2 is done. *Ever.*

✓ Some ideas are genuinely brilliant. *Just... not all of them.*

Final Thought
When to Say Yes (and when to hide the credit card)

Every tradie has that one idea.

Some of them really could make millions.

But before you get swept up in the excitement of another game-changing, world-dominating invention, ask yourself:

Is this the one... or is this just another distraction disguised as genius?

Should I invest my time in a business plan now or just wait?

Because behind every great tradie is a woman rolling her eyes... calculating the costs and keeping the business from going bankrupt over 'the next big thing.'

And if all else fails?

Smile, nod, and remind them to finish the last five 'million-dollar ideas' first.

Chapter 3

'*Hon*, Just Write THE Business Plan for My Genius Invention'

The day my life took an unexpected turn, for life.

Part two of the business planning saga. It started with one sentence. One innocent, five-second request that would unknowingly shape the next thirty-five years of my life and still is.

'Hon, just write a business plan for my invention.'

Not, *'Would you like to be involved in the business?'* or *'Hey, do you want to dedicate the next three decades of your life to this industry?'* No, just a casual *'Whip up a little business plan,'* as if it were the equivalent of jotting down a shopping list.

The invention in question, of course? A sub-arc machine designed to rebuild rollers and idlers for earthmoving track machines. Now, if you're wondering what that means, congratulations! You're already ahead of where I was at the time.

At first, I thought he was just excited about his latest project. After all, most tradies I know have **at least one** world-changing idea *every month*. Our shed is full of them!! That is, the start of project ideas or inventions.

Some want to design a tool that makes their job easier, some want to develop a machine that automates manual labour, and some—like my husband—create complex industrial equipment that could revolutionise an industry sector... an industry sector that was **notorious for not paying their bills by the way.**

Red flag? Oh, absolutely.

But love, as they say, is blind. And in my case, it was also financially optimistic and completely underprepared.

From 'Quick Business Plan' to a Lifetime Commitment

Now, here's the funny thing about business planning. Back then, I knew as much about writing a business plan as I did about rebuilding earthmoving rollers— **which is to say, absolutely nothing.**

But I had heard it's what big businesses do, so I did what any sensible person in my position would do.

I *Googled* it.

Except in the early '90s, **Google didn't exist.**

So, instead, I found myself buried in phone calls, books, connections, and government documents on business planning. I became obsessed with understanding how industries worked, what made businesses succeed (or fail), and how to convince a bank to lend us money without laughing in our faces.

While my husband was focused on building the machine, I was suddenly knee-deep in market research, financial forecasting, pricing strategies, and figuring out who the hell would actually pay for this service.

Let me tell you, **convincing** anyone to part with their money in an industry where 'we'll pay you when we get paid' was a common phrase. **A nightmare.**

The First Business Plan: A Masterpiece of Optimism

Looking back, that first business plan was **equal parts hopeful, delusional, and slightly desperate.** Your first plan is always your worst, they say.

It had **bold revenue projections**, mostly based on the assumption that:

✓ The industry would see the value in our machine.

✓ Customers would actually pay their invoices on time.

✓ We wouldn't go broke within the first six months.

It also had **detailed market research,** which (if I'm being honest) mostly involved calling people and asking, *Would you use this service?* while they muttered something about 'getting back to me' before disappearing forever. Although some of course grabbed hold.

And of course, **it had financial planning**, which, in tradie terms, meant:

'How much will it cost to build this thing?'

'How much do we have in savings?'

'How much do we need to borrow?'

'Can we survive eating baked beans for a while?'

After weeks of studying, writing, rewriting, and faking confidence, the plan was finally complete. It was solid, well-researched, and even had graphs! (Because, obviously, people take you more seriously when you have graphs.)

Then I showed it to my husband.

He skimmed through it, nodded, and said, *'Yeah, looks good. So, when do we start?'*

At that moment, I realised something important. **To him, the plan was just a formality.** The machine was built, the idea was brilliant *(in his mind)*, and the details? **Well, that was my job now.**

Learning Marketing the Hard Way (Without social media!)
Because one size doesn't fit all!?

Marketing isn't a one-trick pony—what works for one business might flop for another. From word-of-mouth and local networking to print ads and strategic partnerships, I learned the hard way that **different audiences need different approaches.** (And yes, this was all before social media took over the world! But even now you need more than just social media)

Once we had a plan, we needed **clients.**

Here's where I had to **teach myself marketing**—and not the easy kind we have today with Facebook ads and Instagram reels. No, I'm talking **1990's marketing:**

- Cold-calling potential clients *(and being 'hung up' on a lot).*

- Driving around with brochures and handing them out at every industrial site that would let me through the gate.

- Newspaper ads *(which cost a fortune).*

- Mailing flyers *(because email marketing wasn't a thing yet).*

- Networking with industry people who only spoke in acronyms.

I quickly discovered that marketing to tradies and industrial businesses was like trying to sell gym memberships to couch potatoes—they knew they needed it, but they didn't want to pay for it.

And let's not forget the finance application process.

Banks in the '90s didn't like risk, and telling them, *'We want to launch a business in an industry full of slow payers!'* didn't exactly inspire confidence.

After pitching, negotiating, and trying not to cry in bank offices, we finally secured some funding.

The machine was ready.

The business was launched.

And I had officially become a **businesswoman.** Even though I still had to take along my husband. In those days, it was not a woman's world with banks either.

Did I expect this to be my career for the next 35 years? **Absolutely not.**

Did my husband realise what he had just signed me up for? Or what I would eventually do for my own business **Also no.**

His Idea, My Life – The Reality of Supporting a Visionary

Over time, I noticed something… interesting.

My husband was brilliant at inventing, fixing, and creating solutions. But when it came to business strategy, financial management, and dealing with clients, that somehow became my role and my business.

It wasn't a conversation. It just... happened.

To him, the business existed because he had the vision. To me, the business existed because **someone had to make it work.**

That 'quick business plan' and business had turned into:

✓   Understanding cash flow, pricing, and expenses.

✓   Tendering processes and negotiation skills with national contractors.

✓   Learning contracts, invoicing, and payment terms (and how to chase money politely).

✓   Becoming a marketing expert, sales rep, and customer service manager.

✓   Managing clients, suppliers, and the occasional dodgy employee.

And, of course, it was always **his invention, his business, his dream**—until something went wrong. Then it was our problem.

Lessons Learned
Writing that First Business Plan Changed Everything

It taught me:

- ✓ Business is 20% vision, 80% execution. 80% mindset and 20% strategy.

- ✓ You can't rely on passion alone—you need strategy.

- ✓ Understanding an industry is just as important as loving what you do.

- ✓ Marketing isn't about being the best; it's about being seen.

- ✓ If you don't plan your finances, you'll always be chasing money.

Final Thought
But the biggest lesson?

If you're not careful, 'helping out' can turn into a full-time career before you even realise it.

And in my case?

Thirty-five years later, I'm still rolling my eyes… but at least I know how to write a damn good business plan. I have written, facilitated and read thousands.

Chapter 4

'We Need 10 Staff for This Job. Yesterday.'

The day my to-do list tripled overnight.

How I became the HR department (without asking for the role). And the nightmare of 'mates' rates and workers who call in sick on Mondays.

There's nothing quite like **winning a massive tender** to make you feel like you're really going places. One day, you're running a business from a small workshop, managing jobs on the go, and the next—**bam!**—you're responsible for delivering two critical fabrication projects for a power station and a wharf.

It was an incredible opportunity. A chance to grow the business, build something on a major industrial scale, and prove that we could handle big contracts.

There was just **one small problem.**

We needed **more people**—fast.

And not just any people. We needed welders and boilermakers who could actually do the job, not just claim they could. Because, as I would soon find out, there's a **huge** difference between holding a welding certificate and *actually knowing what the hell you're doing.*

Of course, while I was knee-deep in recruitment, interviews, and trying to create a hiring process from scratch, Andrew was still happily zipping around doing his mobile repair jobs—because, as he often reminded me, *'I just love fixing different things every day.'*

Meanwhile, I was the one **fixing our workforce issues.**

Hiring Tradies: The Ultimate Crash Course

Now, if you think hiring in today's world is tough, let me tell you—hiring in the '90s was a whole different game.

There was no LinkedIn, no Indeed, no Seek. No one had carefully curated résumés or cover letters written by AI. You put an ad in the newspaper, or Centrelink and whoever read it called you.

And let me tell you, some of the people who applied for these jobs... **were truly something else.**

I learned very quickly that just because someone had a **trade certificate** didn't mean they had:

✓   The ability to actually do the job.

✓   The personality to work well with a team.

✓   Any desire to show up on time *(or at all)*.

So, I had to get smart—**fast.**

I developed a **structured interview process**, something that wasn't really common back then. Most tradie businesses just hired based on:

Tradie-style: Hiring *random blokes* from the pub.

'He's a mate of a mate.'

'Yeah, I think I've heard of him.'

'He's got a welding ticket—should be right.'

But I wanted **better than that.** If we were going to deliver this project properly, we needed people who could actually do the work, **not just talk about it.**

The Interview Process: Separating the Talkers from the Doers

Step one was **advertising**—which, in those days, meant placing an ad in the local paper and waiting for the phone to ring. And ring it did.

I discovered that when hiring tradies, you have to *filter out* the four main types of applicants:

✓ The Overconfident Bullshitter – The guy who claimed he could *'weld anything, anywhere, anytime'* but couldn't strike an arc to save his life.

✓ The Flight Risk – The guy who had *'plenty of experience'* but had switched jobs ten times in three years *(because 'no one appreciated his talent')*.

✓ The Guy Who Just Needed a Job – Not because he loved welding, but *because Centrelink was on his back.*

✓ The friend of the family who should have had the experience but told stories all day *(about Chinook helicopters).*

Once I'd **weeded out** the ones who couldn't actually do the work, I set up **interviews.**

This was where I **really** started rolling my eyes.

Because Andrew and I had very different interviewing styles:

- I asked about experience, problem-solving, teamwork, and reliability.
- Andrew asked about ability and how quickly they could start. That was it.

To his credit, he did get involved in the final decision-making. But his philosophy was simple:

'If they can weld, they're in.'

'If they look like they can work hard, they're in.'

'If they can talk about anything besides Chinook helicopters, they're in.'

Which brings me to our **biggest hiring mistake.**

The Chinook Helicopter Enthusiast: A Cautionary Tale

One of the most valuable *(painful)* lessons I learned during this hiring spree was this:

Just because you know someone from childhood doesn't mean they'll be a good hire.

We thought we were **doing the right thing** by giving someone we'd known for years an opportunity. After all, we knew him, trusted him, and assumed that his trade qualifications meant he'd be a solid worker.

We assumed wrong.

Instead of contributing, he became the workplace storyteller.

Every single day, he would work just long enough stop and start telling long, detailed stories about Chinook helicopters.

What Chinook helicopters had to do with welding formwork for cooling towers, I still don't know. But by the end of his short-lived employment, I could have written a bloody thesis on those things.

Needless to say, we learned our lesson: **hire based on skills**, not on shared childhood memories.

Inductions, Training & Trying to Keep Some Control

Once we had a **team,** I realised we needed more than just people who could weld. We needed **consistency, structure, checks and actual processes.**

So, I did something not many businesses were doing at the time:

- ✓ I created a formal interview process.
- ✓ I developed an induction program so new hires knew what was expected.
- ✓ I wrote training manuals so that everyone followed the same procedures.
- ✓ I set up toolbox meetings with my leading hand
- ✓ And we talked teamwork and culture stuff

At the time, other business owners thought I was going overboard.

'Why bother with training manuals? Just tell or show 'em what to do!'

But I knew we had to operate like a serious business if we wanted to take on more big contracts. Culture and teamwork mattered, and employees forget and need to be reminded and retrained regularly.

And funnily enough, once we had structure, **we started hiring better people.**

The Reality of Managing a Growing Team

Of course, managing staff also came with **new challenges:**

Suddenly, we had a **payroll.**

We had to deal with sick days, no-shows, and *'I forgot to set my alarm.'*

Personal drama somehow became a workplace issue.

One day, I looked around at the team of people I had built, and I realised something:

I wasn't 'just helping' out anymore.

I was running a real business.

And Andrew? He was still out doing mobile repairs, living his best life.

Lessons Learned
What I Wish I'd Known Before Hiring

- ✓ Just because they have a trade certificate doesn't mean they know what they're doing.

- ✓ Hiring mates is risky. If they can't work, you'll lose a friend AND a worker.

- ✓ An interview process isn't 'overkill'—it's necessary.

- ✓ Staff will surprise you—some will step up, and some will disappear the first time it rains.

- ✓ Your husband will always believe *'we'll find someone'* even when you're drowning in job ads.

By the end of our whirlwind hiring spree, we had a **proper team, a growing business, and an ever-expanding list of responsibilities.**

And me?

I was officially **not just *'helping out'* anymore.**

Would I have done things differently if I had known this would become my **life?**

Well... probably. But where's the fun in that?

Remember behind every tradie is a woman rolling her eyes, nodding along, and secretly knowing she's the CEO.

Chapter 5

The Great Divide: Tools vs. Paperwork

When he gets to go do what he loves, like fixing stuff and avoiding paperwork.

Every tradie has **their passion**—whether it's fixing machinery, fabricating steel, or rebuilding something that no one else thought was salvageable.

For Andrew, it was all the above but most of all **getting out of the office and working with his hands.**

For me, well… I never really *chose* my passion.

It just *happened* to be **everything else he didn't want to do.**

And so, while he was out happily welding, repairing, and troubleshooting, I was stuck with the real nuts and bolts of the business:

- ✓ Paperwork
- ✓ Accounting
- ✓ Payroll
- ✓ Scheduling
- ✓ Client management
- ✓ Sorting out supplier dramas
- ✓ Fixing mistakes when someone (not naming names) forgot to file something important

What started as *'Hon, can you just do the …?'* quickly turned into **running an entire full-time business— without the pay.**

Role Clarity

'You Do the Paperwork, I'll Do the Work That Matters'

I think there's a **universal law in tradie businesses** that states: the person who knows how to turn on a computer automatically becomes the office manager.

Andrew wasn't **anti-paperwork**—he just had a *very selective* approach to it. He believed paperwork, diaries and recording things was:

- Boring
- Unnecessary
- Easily ignored until it became urgent

The details were all in his head, and that is what mattered. – a good memory!!

On the other hand, he believed fixing things, designing things, and welding things were:

✓ Exciting

✓ Challenging

✓ Absolutely essential

Which led to **many conversations** that went something like this:

Me: We need to sit down and go through these invoices.

Him: Yep, later.

Me: We need to figure out our finances before the ATO breathes down our necks.

Him: I'll look at it tonight.

Me: Andrew, the tax office does not care that you are busy fixing a hydraulic system.

And yet, somehow, *he still got to do what he loved every day.*

How 'Helping Out' Turned into a Full-Time Office Job

At the beginning, I naively thought I was just **keeping things organised.**

A few invoices here, a few phone calls there—how hard could it be?

But the **tradie business black hole** sucked me in, and before I knew it:

✓ I was handling accounts *(without any formal training).*

✓ I was learning payroll and PAYG tax *(which was harder than it should be).*

✓ I was chasing overdue invoices *(from clients who conveniently disappeared when payment was due)*.

✓ I was negotiating supplier deals *(because tradies will just agree to whatever price they're given)*.

✓ I was fixing quoting mistakes creatively *(like the time 'someone' (cough) underquoted a major job)*.

And, of course, whenever I *tried* to discuss these things with Andrew, his response was always:

'*Hon*, I just want to focus on the work I love doing.'

Which left me standing there, wondering:

Do you know what I love doing? **No?**

Me neither, because I don't get the choice!

The Art of Looking Calm While Internally Screaming

One of my greatest skills (which I mastered during this time) was **pretending to be calm while mentally listing everything that was falling apart.**

Scene: Monday morning

Him: What's on for the week?

Me: Well, we need to submit the next batch of fabrication, finalise payroll, get that equipment order sorted, and call the client about their overdue payment.

Him: Right, well I've got a big repair job today, so can you just handle all that?

Me: (Internally screaming.)

Some days, I thought about **printing out a full business report and leaving it on his service truck seat,** just to see if he'd notice.

Spoiler: He wouldn't have.

When You Handle the Admin, You Hold the Power

At some point, I realised something important:

Behind every tradie is a woman rolling her eyes because she's the real boss, but he doesn't know it yet.

Andrew may have been fixing the machines, welding the steel, and keeping the clients happy on-site, but I was:

✓   Making sure the business actually got paid.

✓   Keeping the tax office from knocking on our door.

✓ Ensuring we didn't run out of supplies.

✓ Handling contracts, agreements, and legal paperwork.

Without me? The business would collapse faster than a dodgy weld.

And *that* is also when I started setting some **ground rules.**

Setting Boundaries: The Key to Survival

I realised if I didn't set **boundaries**, I was going to **spend my life** drowning in business admin while Andrew got to keep doing what he loved.

So, I made a new rule: Every single night at 5:30 pm—after I had bathed the children and made dinner—taken the dinner back into the workshop. Andrew and I would sit down with dinner and plans in hand and go through the business together.

No excuses. No 'I'll look at it later.' This was **non-negotiable.** But hard to keep.

Did he love it? *No.*

Did it work? *Mostly Yes.*

Because suddenly, he started realising **just how much work was involved** in keeping everything afloat.

And more importantly, I changed some of the biggest rules of all:

✓ No more weekend work. *Saturday and Sunday were house and children days.*

✓ No more phone calls during the night *(yes we were a 24/7 business for repairs but you need time out to re charge).*

✓ A proper respect for family time *(because what's the point of working so hard if you never get to enjoy life?)*

✓ No more repair jobs running up on Christmas day *(we installed a locked gate on our property too).*

Did he struggle with it at first? *Oh, absolutely.*

But over time, he saw that by **setting limits**, we weren't just making the business better—**we were making life better.**

Role Clarity

Lessons Learned
Tools Are Great—But So Are Diaries, Dockets & Boundaries

- ✓ If you can turn on a computer and answer the phone without swearing, you're now the business manager. Forever. No takebacks.

- ✓ Andrew had a great memory... but even great memories fade. That's why paperwork, diaries, and written proof beat 'I thought I told you that,' every single time.

- ✓ Tradies will say paperwork is unnecessary... right up until the moment they forget what they promised a client, what steel measurement they needed, or what time they said they'd be home *(spoiler: it wasn't 8 pm)*.

- ✓ No more 'I'll look at it tonight.' Set the meeting. Show up with snacks. And don't be afraid to bring the highlighters and the spreadsheets.

- ✓ Spending time together isn't just for date nights—it's for sitting down with a pile of reports or receipts, a pen, and a 'let's get on the same page' smile that hides mild frustration. And still being best friends at the end of the meeting.

- ✓ If you quietly start printing business reports and highlight major points, then slide them under his nose during smoko... he'll eventually read one. And then (miraculously) he'll start asking questions. *And that, my friends, is how you train a tradie.*

- ✓ Share the load or you'll share the burnout. Taking time to actually understand each other's roles and write job descriptions —his in the shed, yours in the chaos—means fewer arguments and way more 'aha!' moments (and possibly some surprised respect).
- ✓ Admin may not feel exciting, but neither is being audited. One of you gets to fix the machines. The other fixes the future.
- ✓ If the work matters, so does the paperwork. And if you do it right? You'll not only survive the business—you'll *own* it.

Final Thought
The Trade-Offs of a Tradie Business

- ✓ Andrew got to spend his days doing what he loved—working with his hands, fixing things, and building cool stuff.
- ✓ I got to spend my days making sure the business actually functioned.
- ✓ But now, we also get to enjoy weekends, have family time, and actually live our lives.

So yes, behind every great tradie is a woman rolling her eyes... but also making damn sure there's a life outside of work.

Chapter 6

'You Can't Read Plans, But You Can Manage the Project!'

Managing a shed full of tradies while Andrew was off playing with diggers.

If there was one thing Andrew **loved,** it was **machinery breakdowns.** The rush of diagnosing the problem, the satisfaction of getting things running again, the freedom of being out on-site with the big machines—it was his absolute **dream job and it still is at 72.**

And where was I while he was off *having the time of his life?*

Managing a fabrication shed full of 10 - 15 tradesmen, admin staff and a cost estimator... all working on a massive project for a national construction company.

A completely normal situation, *right?*

You know, for someone with **zero formal training in project management, fabrication, or construction.** This is how a wife who *'knows nothing about fabrication'* suddenly becomes the site boss.

But, as I had learned by this point, **logic and fairness do not apply when you're the woman behind the man.**

She doesn't read plans—but she knows the schedule, the staff, and the budget

Let's be clear—I was not **supposed to be in charge** of these fabrication projects.

But Andrew was out **fixing machinery for earthmovers** *(doing what he loved)*, and someone had to **keep the jobs moving.**

And that someone?

Yep. **Me.**

Juggling tradies, suppliers, and clients – while pretending to understand blueprints.

Now, managing 10-15 tradesmen in a fabrication shed **wasn't for the faint-hearted.**

✓ There were welders covered in sparks.

✓ Boilermakers who thought safety glasses were optional.

✓ A cost estimator who *lived* in spreadsheets and refused to round numbers.

Plus the client who told me I had two things between my legs I shouldn't.

And me—standing in the middle of it all, **pretending I had everything under control.**

The thing is, **when you're a woman in a male-dominated space**, people assume you don't know anything about the work.

They don't care if you've:

- ✓ Hired the staff.
- ✓ Set up the contracts.
- ✓ Negotiated the deal.
- ✓ Organised all the materials.
- ✓ Created a damn project timeline.

Nope. All that mattered was that **I wasn't a tradie.**

This meant I got to hear comments like this daily:

'She can't even read the plans—why is she running things?'

To which my internal response was:

'I don't NEED to read the plans, mate—I just need to make sure YOU do.'

But, of course, I had to keep things professional.

So instead, I would just stand there, nod, and confidently point at a deadline on the wall—because the truth is:

If you act like you know what you're doing, people will assume you do.

The Unwritten Rule: 'Just Wait for Andrew'

Now, even though I was running this entire project, there was one **unwritten rule** that I couldn't break:

If a **big decision** needed to be made, everyone would say:

'You have to wait for Andrew for that.'

Oh, really?

Andrew—the guy who was **not here** because he was currently **up to his elbows in hydraulic oil somewhere?**

Andrew—the guy who **trusted me enough to run everything in his absence,** but somehow, that wasn't good enough for everyone else ?

Nope. The moment something went wrong, it was:

'We should probably check with Andrew first.'

Now, I like to think I'm a **reasonable** woman.

But by the **fifth** time I heard this in one day, I had **had enough.**

So, I decided to test something.

The 'Andrew Will Be Back Later' Experiment

One day, after hearing **yet another** *'we should wait for Andrew',* I calmly replied:

'Andrew will be back later, but in the meantime, let's keep moving. If you have any questions, bring them to me.'

And do you know what happened?

They just... did.

Turns out that waiting for Andrew wasn't actually necessary—it was just a **habit.**

Because when the **real boss wasn't around**, they needed **someone to tell them what to do.**

And that person?

Was already me.

When You're 'The Woman Behind the Man'—But Actually Running Everything

One of my **favourite** moments of this whole project was when the **national construction company's project manager called.**

'Can I speak to the person in charge?' he asked.

'You're speaking to her,' I replied.

Silence.

Then:

'Oh... I thought Andrew handled this?'

And THAT was the moment I realised something important:

Even when you are **literally doing all the work, people will assume a man is running things.**

Project management tip: If you sound confident enough, they'll assume you're in charge (because you are).

So, instead of explaining, I just said, 'I've got everything under control. What do you need?'

And guess what?

From that moment on, they **called me directly.**

Lessons Learned
How to Manage a Project When No One Thinks You Can

✓ Confidence is key. If you sound sure of yourself, people will assume you know what you're doing. It's all in your mindset.

✓ Nobody *actually* reads the plans properly anyway. They just pretend they do.

✓ If you make decisions, people will follow them—unless you let them doubt you.

✓ The first time a supplier or client says, 'I thought Andrew was in charge,' simply reply, 'He trusts me to handle it.'

✓ You might never get the official title of 'Project Manager,' but you'll be doing the job anyway.

Final Thought
The Secret to Running a Job Site Without Running Yourself into the Ground

Next Time Someone Says, 'Wait for *Tradie-Husband*,'

Try this:

Smile.

Ask, *'What's the problem?'*

Give a clear solution.

Carry on.

Because if you're already running the show, you might as well own it.

Behind every great tradie is a woman rolling her eyes... and making sure the project actually gets done.

Chapter 7

'Oh My God – Just Do the Job!'

Surviving electricians, parts suppliers, and the never-ending battle against tradie nonsense.

Helen Cowley

The Great Electrical Debate (or how to make a grown woman cry over amps and voltage)

Now, I never set out to become an expert in electrical systems, power loads, or what happens when you mix an unqualified *'she'll be right'* attitude with high-voltage machinery.

But when you run a fabrication business—and need **serious power upgrades**—you end up having conversations with electricians that feel more like an advanced physics exam than a service call.

It all started when we were upgrading our three-phase power to install a high-capacity welder (60 amps) and a press that needed slightly less.

Simple enough, right?

Oh, **how wrong I was.**

Sparky #1: The King of Confusion

The first electrician we called—let's call him *Sparky McBaffle*—showed up, took **one look at me** (not Andrew, ME), and immediately decided that his new mission in life was to **make this as complicated as possible.**

'Ah, well, you see, the thing about three-phase power is that it's all about the resistance load, which, in turn, is affected by the impedance of the system, and of course, we need to consider your peak voltage fluctuations relative to your power factor—'

Excuse me.

What?

I nodded, as if I understood, and asked:

'So... can you install the 60-amp circuit for the welder?'

He smirked.

'Well, see, that depends on your kVA rating and whether your transformer can handle the reactive power without tripping the neutral load.'

I stared.

'Okay... but can you install it?'

'Yeah, nah, we'd have to check your phase balancing across your switchboard. Might take a few weeks to do a proper assessment.'

A few weeks?

For a simple power upgrade?

This was not brain surgery.

This was 'install the bloody circuit so we can run the machines.'

Sparky #2: The Actual Professional

At this point, I knew what I had to do—**find someone who could cut the crap and just do the job.**

Enter Sparky #2, a no-nonsense, 50-something electrician who arrived, **took one look at our setup**, and said:

'You need 60 amps for the welder, press needs a little less, yeah?'

'Yes!'

He nodded, walked over to the switchboard, checked a few things, and within five minutes, gave me a straight answer.

'Yep, easy fix. We'll run a new breaker, upgrade your isolator, and get it sorted. Should be done by Wednesday.'

No lecture.

No mystery.

No unnecessary delay.

Just the job done.

By the time he left, I felt **seen**.

Ladies, if you ever find a tradie who does the job without a performance piece worthy of an Oscar, treasure them.

They are rarer than a **full set of matching Tupperware lids.**

Ordering Parts: The Left-Handed Screwdriver Special

Now, dealing with electricians was one thing.

But ordering parts as a woman in a tradie business?

That was next-level painful.

The Great Hardware Store Initiation

If you've never had the joy of walking into a **male-dominated hardware supply store as a woman looking for specific parts**, let me paint you a picture.

I'd be sent to pick up bolts, nuts, seals, bearings—the stuff that kept our machines running.

So, naturally, I'd walk up to the counter, **order what we needed,** and wait.

And almost **every single time,** the bloke behind the counter would exchange a smirk with his coworker before engaging in a little game I like to call *'Let's Confuse the Woman.'*

'Are you sure you don't need a left-handed screwdriver with that?'

'Did he say he wanted fine-threaded or coarse-threaded? Might make a difference.'

'You know, those seals won't work if your bore size is off by even a fraction of a millimetre.'

Now, these men weren't **asking for useful details.**

They were **testing me.**

Waiting for me to get flustered.

Waiting for me to say, *'Oh, I don't know, I'll have to check,'* so they could roll their eyes, shake their heads, and mutter something about *'the wife doing the ordering'* as if that was some kind of crime.

The Solution: Bulletproof Orders and Zero Small Talk

After one too many *'do you want the metric or imperial version?'* traps, I wised up.

I started doing two things:

1. **I sent detailed purchase orders via fax**—part numbers, specs, and a note that said, 'No substitutions without prior approval.'

2. **I stopped engaging in their games.**

The next time I walked into the store and some guy smirked at me and said,

'Are you sure that's the right bearing size? Could be a tricky one.'

I smiled sweetly and replied,

'Well, unless physics has changed overnight, I'm pretty damn sure.'

Silence.

Order filled in **record time.**

Lessons Learned
Tradies Love to Test You—But You Don't Have to Play

✓ If an electrician starts throwing unnecessary jargon at you, just ask: 'Can you install it, yes or no?'

✓ If they hesitate, find someone else.

✓ When ordering parts, avoid unnecessary conversation—just send the order and collect.

✓ Men in hardware stores will try to mess with you, but a confident response shuts them up fast.

✓ Efficiency is a skill few tradespeople master—when you find one who has, never let them go.

Final Thought
The Day I Stopped Playing the Game

There was a time when I let people talk down to me, waste my time, and test my patience.

But somewhere between electrical nightmares and hardware store shenanigans, I realised something:

I didn't have to **prove myself** to anyone.

I just had to **get the job done.**

So now, when someone tries to **overcomplicate, confuse, or undermine me,** I just smile and say:

'Look, mate, I'm not here for a lecture—I'm here for a solution. Can you do the job, or should I find someone who actually can?'

And behind every great tradie is a woman rolling her eyes... because she's already five steps ahead.

Chapter 8

'I'll Just Pop in and Tell You What You Did Wrong'

The 5:30 pm debrief: A daily exercise in patience.

The daily family business meeting *(Performance Review)*, which you never asked for.

Every day at 5:30 pm sharp, *like clockwork*, Andrew would return to the workshop after a long day of doing what he loved—fixing, welding, and problem-solving out in the field.

And every day, *like clockwork*, I would have already sprinted out the door to pick up the kids from childcare, bathe them, throw dinner together at lightning speed, and then race back to the workshop so we could have our *5:30 pm daily partner toolbox meeting*.

This was the time when we would—**in theory**—review the day's progress, discuss what had gone well, and calmly work through any issues.

In reality?

It was a **45-minute critique session** where Andrew would *pop in* and systematically **tell me everything I did wrong.**

Feedback & Communication

Welcome to the 'What You Missed' Review

Now, let's be clear.

By 5:30 pm, **I had already worked a full day,** handled staff issues, juggled suppliers, managed project deadlines, fielded phone calls from the national construction company, and **ensured nobody set fire to the shed** *(which, believe me, was a genuine risk some days).*

And yet, the second Andrew **stepped back onto the workshop floor,** his built-in **Tradie Radar** would scan the entire project like a high-tech security system, instantly detecting **every single thing** that wasn't *exactly* how he would have done it.

Within minutes, the daily **Performance Review** would begin:

'Why did we order this material instead of that one?'

'Who set up this section like this? It's all wrong.'

'Why did we go with that supplier? They're slow as hell.'

'Did no one check this measurement?'

Now, keep in mind—**he had not been there all day.**

He had **not** spoken to the suppliers, the client, or the team.

He had **not** dealt with the paperwork, scheduling, or childcare pickup sprint.

But none of that mattered because his **tradie instincts** had kicked in, and suddenly, he knew exactly what needed fixing, and what was wrong with the plan the supplier draftsmen had sent.

How to respond when he says, 'Why didn't you do it this way?'

At this point, I had three choices:

- Listen and learn about plans and what all the jargon meant.

- Defend my decisions and explain all the logical reasons why things were done the way they were.

- Smile, nod, and mentally add 'revenge' to tomorrow's to-do list.

I usually went with option one while practicing deep breathing instead of throwing the laptop at his head. After all, you never know everything. There is always something new every day.

Feedback & Communication

The Time He Argued with the Draftsman (and won?!)

One of my *favourite* toolbox sessions (and by *favourite*, I mean *deeply frustrating but also hilarious in hindsight*) was the day Andrew **went to war with the lead draftsman** of the large construction company we were working with.

The issue?

One of the work platform installations wasn't spaced far enough apart; it was 50cm.

Now, I had already raised this concern earlier in the week. I had checked the drawings, I had spoken to the team, and the draftsman himself had told me that the placement was correct according to the plans.

End of discussion, right?

Not with Andrew.

He took **one look** at the setup, furrowed his brow, and declared, *'That's not right.'*

Now, the draftsman—who had been in the industry for decades—**immediately disagreed.**

And that's when things got interesting.

What followed was a 30-minute standoff where two grown men argued over measurements, physics, and the proper spacing of industrial platforms.

It was the unstoppable force of *Tradie Gut Instinct* versus the immovable object of *Qualified Engineering Logic.*

And just when I thought I was going to have to physically drag Andrew away before things escalated into a full-blown whiteboard war, the draftsman sighed and said:

'Fine. Let's construct this part in the yard'

And wouldn't you know it?

Andrew. Was. **Right.**

One platform was over the top of another – no way could anyone stand on the lower.

And do you think he was humble about this discovery?

Absolutely not.

Instead, he turned to me, grinned, and said, 'See? This is why you don't trust draftsmen over a bloke with a tape measure.'

And that's when I realised that no matter how many plans, contracts, or official blueprints we followed, Andrew would always, *always* **trust his gut first. And so should I.**

The Art of Pretending to Take Feedback While Planning Revenge

One of the greatest skills I developed during these daily debriefs was the ability to look calm while mentally plotting my revenge.

Because, let's be honest—when you've handled the entire day's workload, then bathed kids and cooked dinner, only to be hit with a lecture on *'what you could have done better,'* you are not in the mood for constructive criticism.

So, instead of arguing, I developed a four-step survival strategy:

Step 1: The Blank Stare

Maintain eye contact.

Nod occasionally.

Think about whether we still have ice cream in the freezer.

Step 2: The 'Interesting Point' Response

Say things like: *'That's a good point.'*

Follow it up with *'I'll make a note of that.'*

Make no actual notes.

Step 3: The Tactical Redirect

Casually ask, *'So, how did your breakdown repair go today?'*

Let him launch into a 20-minute story about his heroic efforts fixing an excavator in record time.

Smile. Escape toolbox review unscathed.

Step 4: The Revenge Plot

Tomorrow, when he asks for a minor admin favour, dramatically sigh and say, *'Oh, sorry, I would have done that, but I didn't want to make another mistake.'*

Watch him look confused.

Smile sweetly.

Because business is business and work is work, but at some stage, you have to plot revenge, have a real conversation, and carve out a life beyond it all.

Feedback & Communication

Lessons Learned
How to Survive the 5:30 pm Performance Review

- ✓ Tradie instinct will always overrule engineering logic. just accept it.

- ✓ If a man has a tape measure in his hand, he is automatically an expert in everything.

- ✓ No matter how much work you've done, there will always be a *'why didn't you do it this way?'* discussion.

- ✓ When in doubt, let him tell his own story about his *'big win'* for the day—it's an excellent distraction tactic.

- ✓ If you can't beat them, outlast them.

- ✓ Plot your life beyond your business.

Final Thought
The Power of Selective Listening

By the time we had finished our nightly toolbox meetings, I had become an expert in selective listening.

I knew that, deep down, Andrew wasn't trying to criticise me—he was just wired to problem-solve.

And while I rolled my eyes through every single one of his 'suggestions,' I also knew that at the end of the day:

✓ The business was running smoothly.

✓ The projects were getting done.

✓ We were still a team (even if one got *more credit* than the other).

✓ At the end of a meeting, you have life and love.

So yes, every great tradie will pop in to tell you what you did wrong...

But behind every great tradie is a woman who smiles, nods, and secretly runs the whole damn show anyway rolling her eyes.

Chapter 9

'You're Not Fired Until a Man Says So!'

Surviving HR in a tradie world where no one thinks you're the boss.

Helen Cowley

Congratulations, You're Now the Entire HR Department!

If you've ever wondered how someone with zero HR experience ends up running recruitment, training, workplace health & safety, and performance management in a male-dominated industry, let me introduce you to my life.

One minute, I was *helping out* by handling a bit of admin.

The next minute?

I was writing employment contracts, designing training programs, and trying to figure out how to fire someone who refused to believe I had the authority to do so.

Because, as I quickly discovered, **you're not REALLY fired until a man says so.**

Hiring Tradies: A Masterclass in Filtering Out the 'Know-it-Alls'

When we landed bigger projects, we needed more staff—which meant I had to learn how to recruit.

At first, I was **optimistic**.

I imagined hiring skilled, hardworking professionals who took pride in their craft.

What I got was:

✓ Blokes who rocked up late to the interview... for a job requiring 6 am starts.

✓ Guys who claimed they had 'years of experience' but couldn't hold a tape measure properly.

✓ One fellow who spent the entire interview talking about his weekend 'Chinook' trip.

✓ A tradesman who literally asked, 'What exactly does this job involve?'—AFTER APPLYING FOR IT.

✓ And those that couldn't take direction from a woman.

So, I had to **get smart.**

I started screening people like a bouncer at a dodgy nightclub:

✓ If you showed up **without steel caps?** NO ENTRY.

✓ If you referred to your last boss as *'that dickhead'*? NO ENTRY.

✓ If you told me you were *'a quick learner'* but had no relevant skills? NO ENTRY.

✓ And I leave the rest to your imagination...

The Realisation: Just Because They Have a Ticket Doesn't Mean They Know What They're Doing

Once I **finally** managed to hire a **half-decent team**, I had another **shocking discovery**—just because someone had a **trade qualification** didn't mean they knew how to **actually do the job properly or weld.**

I assumed that, since they were qualified, they would know how to operate expensive welding and fabrication equipment and look after it too.

Ha! Cute.

Enter **The Subarc Disaster.**

The Tradie Who Couldn't Weld (and Refused to Listen to a Woman Who Could)

By this stage, I had learned about different types of welders, eg MIG, TIG, and Subarc. Plus to recognise good from bad welding – *the splatter approach.*

I could use and manage our 1000kg capacity rotator with a Subarc and 100-ton press machinery. I knew how to make a good weld and what to do if something went wrong. I rebuilt 100's of idlers and rollers. I knew how it worked. I understood the settings. I could see when someone was wasting material or messing up (meaning it needed to be ground back to re-build).

This brings me to one particularly infuriating employee.

He was a trained tradesman, he had the certification, and yet, every time he knew better than *me*.

However he used to:

- ✓ Waste the flux material.
- ✓ Leave dodgy welds that needed to be reworked.
- ✓ And, started damaging the actual equipment.

So, being the **responsible manager** I had now become, I pulled him aside and gave him **some instruction.**

Him: Oh yeah, yeah, I got it.

(Spoiler: He did not, in fact, *'got it.'*)

The **next time** I saw him using the machine, he was doing the **exact same thing.**

So, I gave him **another** warning.

Me: Mate, you need to adjust the settings. You're blowing through too much wire and wasting flux.

Him: Ah yeah, yeah, I know, I know.

(Turns out, *'I know'* actually means *'I will continue doing exactly what I was doing before.'*)

Third warning.

Me: Okay, this is your last chance. If you keep ignoring instructions, you're done.

Him: Yeah, yeah, all good.

The next day?

Same thing.

So, **I fired him.**

Did he leave?

No.

Instead, he looked at me **dead in the eyes.**

Him: I'll just wait until Andy gets back and see if he'll fire me too.

OH. OH, YOU THINK SO?!

At that moment, I experienced **rage so intense I briefly left my body.**

But instead of **losing my mind**, I simply walked out to find Andrew, who had just returned from a machinery breakdown job.

Me: If you override my decision, YOU can do all the hiring, training, and payroll from now on

Andrew **blinked** at me, turned to the now-very-arrogant tradie, and said:

'Mate, if she fired you, that's it. Pack up.'

Victory.

And FINALLY, **people stopped assuming they had to wait for Andrew to confirm my decisions.**

Why Do My Eyes Roll? Let Me Count the Reasons…

By this stage, my **eye-rolls had reached Olympic levels.**

Why? Because I had spent years:

✓ Explaining why employment contracts actually matter.

✓ Writing training manuals so people wouldn't destroy expensive equipment.

✓ Trying (and failing) to get certain men to take instructions from a woman.

✓ Realising one bad apple can change your culture, so stand up for the culture you want.

✓ Just fire if they won't listen to instructions after THREE TIMES, too bad if he didn't believe I had the authority.

So yes, when people say *'HR is easy,'* I roll my eyes.

When someone says *'Just hire a few blokes, it'll be fine,'* I roll my eyes.

And when I hear *'I'll just wait for Andy to get back,'* I roll my eyes **so hard I almost see my own brain.**

Lessons Learned
How to Survive HR in a Tradie Business

- ✓ Hiring is like fishing—you have to throw back a lot of bad catches before you find a good one.

- ✓ Training manuals are essential—otherwise, someone will ruin your expensive equipment or themselves

- ✓ If you fire someone, make sure they actually leave.

- ✓ If they have a good attitude, you can work with them.

- ✓ Culture matters. Attitude matters.

- ✓ Always listen and learn—even your tradesman who knows more than you.

- ✓ At some point, you either take full control, or you spend your life waiting for someone else.

Human Resources Challenges

Final Thought
Owning My Role (Whether they liked it or not)

By the time I had hired, trained, and cycled through more employees than I cared to count, I had a realisation:

I wasn't just *helping out*.

I wasn't *the woman behind the man*.

I was **HR, crisis management, and a full-time babysitter in disguise.**

And if anyone dared to question that?

Let's just say, I'd mastered the art of hiring, firing, and filtering out the blokes who thought *'rocking up most days'* counted as reliability.

Behind every great tradie isn't just a woman rolling her eyes… she's the one making sure the wrong hires don't turn every job site into a disaster zone.

Tradie Talk: *Welding Splatter refers to the small, molten droplets of metal that are splashed or scattered during the welding process, forming unsightly globules and potentially causing burns.*

Chapter 10

'We Don't Really Need Staff Living With Us... Do We?'

The accidental apprentice adoption program and other business mistakes. Lesson number 365, which should be lesson number one.

How We Became an Unofficial Halfway House

At some point in our business journey, we accidentally became a boarding house for wayward tradies.

It started innocently enough—one of the apprentices had nowhere to stay for a few nights while he sorted himself out.

'*Hon*, it's just for a couple of nights,' Andrew said.

A couple of nights.

Oh, how **naïve I was.**

Because one apprentice turned into two, and then suddenly we had a rotating cast of tradesmen who had somehow convinced themselves that our house was a free accommodation service for employees in need.

At one point, I half-expected to wake up and find a full site crew eating breakfast at my kitchen table.

And do you think **Andrew saw a problem with this?**

Absolutely not.

'They're all good blokes! They just need a hand, or a place to stay,' he'd say.

Meanwhile, I was **running a steel fabrication business, raising a family, and now—apparently—managing a bloody hostel.**

When Your Staff Are Your Drinking Buddies, You've Got a Problem

Now, let's talk about the fundamental problem with treating staff like mates.

Andrew loved his team.

He loved having a beer with them after work.

He loved helping them out whenever they were struggling.

He loved being their mate, not just their boss.

But do you know what's awkward?

When the bloke you were drinking with on Saturday night is the same bloke you have to discipline on Monday morning.

When you're **too emotionally involved**, making business decisions becomes **ten times harder.**

Because suddenly, it's not:

✓ *'This person isn't performing well—time to let them go.'*

It's:

- ✗ 'But his missus just left him, and he's having a tough time.'
- ✗ 'Yeah, he stuffed up, but he's a good bloke—I'll give him another chance.'
- ✗ 'I can't fire him; he helped us build the shed three years ago!'

This is how **underperforming staff stick around for far too long.**

Why We Needed to Draw the Line (And why it took so long)

At first, I tried **gently** suggesting that maybe—just maybe—we needed to establish some boundaries.

Me: Andrew, staff are employees, not housemates.

Andrew: Yeah, yeah, I know.

Me: Andrew, we cannot keep feeding the apprentices.

Andrew: Ah, it's just a meal, *Hon*.

Me: Andrew, I am not running a free crisis accommodation centre.

Andrew: It's only temporary!

Newsflash: **It was never temporary.**

We had *mates* staying around for weeks when we only agreed for two weeks.

Seven months. I was done!

And then, we found ourselves calling an ambulance for a mate who accidentally caught his work shirt on fire for the third time.

That was it.

We had to have a hard discussion about best mates and the separation of employees and family.

'That's it!' I declared. *'We need LINES IN THE SAND!'*

Because **staff are staff.**

Mates are mates.

Business is business.

And if you **blur that line too much,** you will:

✓ Get taken advantage of.

✓ Lose authority in your own business.

✓ Struggle to make **tough but necessary** business decisions.

And just like that, our **Accidental Apprentice Adoption Program** was officially **shut down.**

Lessons Learned
Staff Are Not Your Mates

✓ If you let one staff member stay 'just for a few nights,' you'll wake up one day running an unofficial halfway house.

✓ Drinking with employees is fun... until you have to discipline them on Monday morning.

✓ If you keep bailing out staff financially, congratulations—you're now a charity, not a business. We all like to help, but draw the line somewhere.

✓ Your home is not an extension of your workshop. If an apprentice eats cereal in his undies at your kitchen table, you've lost control.

✓ At some point, you either draw the line or accept that your business (and personal life) is now one giant mess.

Final Thought
Why I Now Fantasise About an Off-Grid Retreat

After years of balancing work, staff, and an unintentional live-in tradie program, I now have a new dream.

It's not about business expansion or making millions.

It's about moving to an off-grid retreat where no staff members can find me.

Because, as much as I love building a successful business, I also love not waking up to a fully grown man in my kitchen, wearing nothing but boxers and a bad hangover.

So yes, behind every great tradie is a woman rolling her eyes... and enforcing bloody boundaries.

Chapter 11

We Didn't Make a Profit, But We Have All the Excuses

How I learned that cash flow is king (and that lawyers are surprisingly useful).

Helen Cowley

Where Did the Money Go? (Hint: It wasn't profit)

At some point in our business journey, I started noticing a **frustrating pattern.**

We would pay everyone and everything first and guess what – what was left was our pay.

We'd finish a big field job or tender, that had been quoted or done within performance hours, send out the part payment claims or invoices, and eagerly wait for the **sweet, sweet arrival of our well-earned money.**

And then...

Nothing.

No money. No payment. Just a bunch of **very creative excuses.**

There are three parts to this story: the moving client holding up invoice payments, the contractor changing rules, and our own expense excuses for the new widget toys that we just had to have.

My favourite saying is,' You can make excuses or you can change things, but you can't do both'.

There are different versions of this too:

'You can make excuses or you can make money, but you can't do both'

I will start with our own excuses:

And every single time, I'd hear the same things from Andrew:

- ✓ 'The client was a nightmare.'
- ✓ 'The supplier overcharged us.'
- ✓ 'We just needed that new welder, *Hon*.'

Oh yes.

The *mysterious disappearance of profit* was **never our fault.**

No, no. It was **always something else.**

IT IS YOUR BUSINESS, YOUR EXCUSES AND YOUR ADAPTABILITY to change and think differently that matter.

And that, dear reader, is also how I learned that tradies are brilliant problem-solvers... until the problem is financial.

The Great Cash Flow Catastrophe

Now, I was never expected to be a financial genius.

But after one too many *'Where the hell did our money go?'* moments, I realised something:

It's not just about how much money you make—it's about how much you actually keep.

And that's when I started learning about cash flow much deeper.

And do you know what I discovered?

Large contractors do not care about paying you on time. Particularly if you let them – no policies yourself.

Not only do they **ignore the payment terms** they agreed to, but they also:

✓ Change them if they think they can get away with it.

✓ Suddenly need to *'run it past accounting'* (which apparently takes six to eight weeks).

✓ Disappear the moment you try to follow up.

✓ Magically find a 'discrepancy' on the invoice.

Meanwhile, we had **wages, suppliers, rent, and oh yeah—actual lives to pay for.**

And yet, Andrew's solution to this was…

'We just have to be patient, 'Hon. They'll pay eventually- their good blokes.'

EXCUSE ME?

Patience does not pay the bills.

Patience does not stop the **phone calls from suppliers wondering where their money is.**

Patience does not **magically refill the bank account** after we've spent all our cash reserves.

I realised we needed **real strategies.**

That's how I learned about **reverse planning.**

Reverse Planning: The Financial Trick That Saved My Sanity

Before this, our financial planning looked something like this:

- Do the work.
- Send the invoice.
- Hope for the best.

Shocking that this method didn't work, *right?*

So, I started planning backward.

Instead of hoping we'd make a profit, I built a plan that made **profit non-negotiable.**

Here's how it worked:

✓   We set our profit FIRST. Before a single job was quoted, I determined exactly how much profit we needed to make. That was above our own pay!!

✓   We set budgets as a percentage, not just dollar amounts. This meant expenses couldn't just 'blow out' because we were tracking them properly too.

✓   We accounted for slow payers. If we knew a client had a reputation for paying late, we factored delays into our cash flow projections.

✓   We actually saved for tax (Yes, this is a lesson you can learn the hard way).

And suddenly?

The *'mystery of the missing money'* was solved. We had more control, and things changed immediately from a loss to 30% profit.

Cash Flow Management

How to Handle Clients Who Think 30 Days Means 'Whenever I Feel Like It '

One of the biggest struggles in small business? **Clients who treat payment terms as a vague suggestion.**

At first, we ran on standard 30-day terms. Then reality hit—30 days turned into 60, then 90, and suddenly, we were basically giving out **interest-free loans** while trying to keep our own cash flow afloat.

So, after one too many 'Oh, we'll process that next week' excuses, we made a change:

✓   Invoices now due in 7 days.

✓   No payment, no more work. Simple.

Yes, we lost a few clients in the short term. But here's the thing—**if you're good at your trade, they come back.** The ones who disappeared? They were probably never going to pay on time anyway.

And for the truly difficult payers—the ones who bounce cheques like it's a sport? That's where **machinery leverage** comes in. If you can't pay, your equipment stays put. Would you believe that suddenly, payments got a whole lot faster?

Lesson learned: **Cash flow is king, and leverage is a beautiful thing.**

Lawyers Aren't Just for Rich People (or big problems)

Another painful discovery! Use the experts.

Contracts mean nothing if you don't enforce them.

We had signed contracts that clearly stated payment terms.

And yet, when a big contractor refused to pay, we'd hear things like:

- ✓ *'Oh, we're still waiting on a few approvals.'*
- ✓ *'It's in processing—just give it a few more weeks.'*
- ✓ *'We're having some internal delays.'*
- ✓ *'We thought you'd just roll it into the next job.'*

And my personal favourite:

- ✓ Or payment is on delivery and *'we now don't want our last delivery for 12 months,'* so not only did we have to store what we had manufactured on their schedule, we were to store and wait for payment!!!!!!!

WHAT?!

So, after **one too many polite phone calls that led nowhere,** we finally did something radical:

We got a lawyer.

And let me tell you—**he was our very own David against Goliath.**

He sent **one** strongly worded letter.

One.

Magically, the payment that *'was going to be held for 12 months'* only took another month. And another that had been *'stuck in processing'* for months suddenly **appeared in our account.**

I was equal parts furious and overjoyed.

Furious because why did it take a lawyer for them to pay what they already owed us?!

Overjoyed because we had finally cracked the code.

The lesson?

If you're dealing with a corporate Goliath, don't waste time chasing them—just call a David with a law degree.

Specialist have their place in your business.

The Machinery Widget that 'Was Definitely Necessary'

Now, I would love to tell you that, after all this learning, Andrew (and I sometimes) suddenly became financial wizards.

But no.

Because just when I thought we were **finally getting our cash flow under control**, Andrew came home one day and proudly announced:

'*Hon*, I got a new...!'

A NEW machinery widget.

Because, according to him, '*We needed it.*'

Now, do you want to know what's **hilarious** about that?

At no point in our **reverse planning, budget meetings, or financial discussions** had we ever said, '*We should definitely spend a huge amount of cash on a new...*'

I am sure that, as a tradie's wife or partner, you have heard the stories of the 'man toys', well it is not different in this business or household!!

But Andrew, bless his tradie heart, believed that **business success = new toys.**

And so, just like that, we had a **brand new toy and a slightly thinner bank account.**

Cash Flow Management

(But hey, at least it was tax deductible.)

Lessons Learned

How to Stop Making Excuses and Start Making Profit

✓ Set profit FIRST, then work backward. If you don't plan for profit, you won't have any.

✓ Large contractors play games with money—learn the rules and fight back.

✓ Don't wait for clients to 'do the right thing.' Get a lawyer.

✓ Never release a machine until the payment has cleared. No exceptions.

✓ Set your own terms of payment - and stick to them . Use them like a bible.

✓ If your husband says, 'We needed that new toy' demand receipts—no ask him to budget for it, not just come home with it.

✓ Excuses don't pay the bills—cash flow planning does.

Final Thought
No More Excuses, Just Better Planning

After years of learning the hard way, I finally understood that profit **isn't something that just happens—it's something you plan for and control.**

And now?

Whenever Andrew tries to tell me **why** we *'didn't make as much as expected,'* I simply hold up our reverse planning sheet and say:

'That's nice, *Hon*. Now, where exactly did the money go?'

Because behind every great tradie is a woman rolling her eyes… and keeping the business financially in control and alive.

THIS IS WHY YOU NEED A DIRECT LINE TO A LAWYER, AN ACCOUNTANT, AND A THERAPIST.

And honestly? These days, you might as well throw in a business coach, a support group, and a fully stocked wine fridge while you're at it.

Chapter 12

Lockable Gates & Learning to Say No

Because stakeholder communication is an art form, and sometimes, it needs a padlock.

Where Communication Meets Chaos...

You know that moment when your partner casually says, *'Hon, can you just take/make the calls?'*

And before you know it, you're the voice of the business—shaping client relationships, crafting marketing messages, setting the tone with suppliers, managing expectations, smoothing over project hiccups, and somehow turning emails and newsletters into loyalty-building gold. You're building a brand, not just sending updates. You're turning service into reputation. And you're doing it all between phone calls, family dinners, and the occasional 'love letter' that keeps customers coming back for more.

Because let's face it—when you're the one doing the talking, the listening, the follow-up and the fixing...

you're not just helping out. You're building the whole damn business brand.

Yep. Me too.

This chapter isn't about being the CEO (though let's be honest, I basically was).

It's about drawing the line in the dirt—then redrawing it in hazard tape, wet paint, and finally installing a steel gate with a padlock and a polite but firm sign...because

Chapter 12

Lockable Gates & Learning to Say No

Because stakeholder communication is an art form, and sometimes, it needs a padlock.

Where Communication Meets Chaos...

You know that moment when your partner casually says, *'Hon, can you just take/make the calls?'*

And before you know it, you're the voice of the business—shaping client relationships, crafting marketing messages, setting the tone with suppliers, managing expectations, smoothing over project hiccups, and somehow turning emails and newsletters into loyalty-building gold. You're building a brand, not just sending updates. You're turning service into reputation. And you're doing it all between phone calls, family dinners, and the occasional 'love letter' that keeps customers coming back for more.

Because let's face it—when you're the one doing the talking, the listening, the follow-up and the fixing...

you're not just helping out. You're building the whole damn business brand.

Yep. Me too.

This chapter isn't about being the CEO (though let's be honest, I basically was).

It's about drawing the line in the dirt—then redrawing it in hazard tape, wet paint, and finally installing a steel gate with a padlock and a polite but firm sign...because good communication builds strong relationships, but great boundaries keep them that way.

When you don't set boundaries and communicate, someone will turn up at your front door on Christmas morning asking for an *'emergency'* repair.

And someone else *(ahem, your husband)* will probably say,

'I'll just take a quick look.'

It's not just survival—it's **growth.**

Because I also learned that great communication isn't just about avoiding burnout—

It's the key to building trust, loyalty, and **clients who don't price shop you every five minutes.**

Welcome to the Christmas Day Wake-Up Call From Hell

One of the *great joys* of my role was **handling client requests.**

Now, you might assume that **business hours exist for a reason.**

You would be **wrong.**

Because in the **tradie world**, some clients believe that:

✓ Christmas Day is a perfectly reasonable time to rock up at your front door asking for repairs.

✓ Weekends are just another workday (whether you like it or not).

✓ If you don't answer immediately, you must be dead—or at the very least, being deliberately difficult. – So, I will just turn up at your door!

And that is how, one **Christmas morning**, just as we were settling in to enjoy some family time, we heard a loud truck roll in past our house on the way to our shed.

The Christmas Day Surprise Customer

Now, I don't know what normal people expect to find at their front gate on Christmas morning—perhaps a **caroller, a friendly neighbour, or maybe even Santa himself.**

What I did not expect was a grumpy-looking earthmover operator standing there in his work boots and high-vis vest.

And do you think he had a **Merry Christmas greeting?**

Nope.

Instead, he waved his arm in the direction of his machine and said:

'G'day. Any chance you can fix this?'

Excuse me?!

It was **Christmas Day.**

A day of family, food, and not thinking about work.

A day when **even the most hardcore tradies should know that turning up at someone's home unannounced is a bold move.**

Yet, here he was—standing at our door, looking genuinely confused as to why I might not be thrilled about discussing hydraulic repairs between bites of my Christmas ham.

The Negotiation (That Shouldn't Have Been Necessary)

I took a deep breath and tried **diplomacy.**

'Mate, it's Christmas.'

To which he replied, completely unfazed,

'Yeah, I know, but she's playing up again, and I really need her running by tomorrow.'

For context, *'she'* was his machine, not his wife.

Yes, this man was so committed to his earthmoving equipment that he spent Christmas morning trying to get it serviced.

I blinked.

Was this really happening?

I tried again.

'We're actually closed today. It's family time.'

His response?

'Ah, yeah, fair enough. But if you could just take a quick look—'

QUICK LOOK?!

I glanced at Andrew, hoping for backup.

But do you think my dear, sweet husband, *my partner in business and life*, was going to say no to a fellow earthmover and tinkering with a machine?

Of course not.

Instead, he shrugged and said:

'I'll just have a quick look, Hon'

Behind every tradie is a woman rolling her eyes... because she knew this was coming.

Client Boundaries

Lessons Learned
Setting Boundaries in a Business That Never Sleeps

- ✓ Some clients believe Christmas Day is an appropriate time for regular repairs.

- ✓ If your husband is also a tradie, he will always take their side and tinker.

- ✓ Saying 'no' is a skill you must master—preferably before someone rocks up at your house on a public holiday.

- ✓ If you don't set boundaries, you'll spend your life explaining to people why your personal time is not their business hours.

- ✓ Tradies are committed to their machines—sometimes more than their actual families.

Final Thought
The Day I Started Locking the Front Gate

After that Christmas morning, I made one of those important changes:

We installed a big steel lockable front gate.

Because behind every great tradie is a woman rolling her eyes... and learning to set some damn boundaries.

Chapter 13

Love Letters and Tracking Calls

Because suppliers magically change their stories.

Another one of those most **important lessons I learned** was that if you don't **document everything,** including calls, suppliers will *magically forget what they promised you.*

if you've ever had a supplier change their story mid-job, you'll know this one:

For example, a supplier might say:

'The parts will be here by Friday.'

Then Friday comes, and suddenly:

'Oh no, we said next Friday.'

Or worse:

'We never agreed to that price.'

OH, BUT I WROTE IT DOWN, MATE.

So, I started tracking every single call. And documenting my phone discussions and agreements. My phone book records have got us out of a number of difficult times.

And do you know what happened?

MAGICALLY, the supplier will 'find a way' to give you the right price they told you in the first place.

Funny how a **written record** can trigger supplier amnesia recovery.

Even funnier how quickly pricing *'mistakes'* get fixed when you start forwarding call summaries with subject lines like:

'Just confirming our agreement (again).'

Whether you're talking to customers or chasing quotes, **communication isn't a luxury—it's a power tool.**

Use it well, and you build a reputation for being on the ball, in control.

Always. Track. Everything.

Newsletters: AKA Client 'Love Letters '

Now, because I had somehow become the entire marketing department, I decided to start sending out regular newsletters to our clients, similar to newsletters and surveys, that you most probably do now. I also designed and set surveys.

Nothing flashy.

A little update here, a quick project highlight there. Maybe a reminder about lead times, and *(if I had time to be fancy)* a tip or two about maintaining equipment between jobs.

And when I got brave, I even added a short survey, with a **teabag attached** and a note that said:

'Put the kettle on, and tell us what you think.'

Now, did I expect responses?

Not really.

Did I expect *construction company owners and grumpy foremen* to actually read them?

Absolutely not.

But guess what?

They did.

And do you know what these tough tradies called them?

'Your regular love letters.'

At first, I wasn't sure whether to be **flattered or concerned.**

But then I realised something **brilliant:**

These 'love letters' meant they **remembered us.**

- ✓ They were connection points
- ✓ Little nudges that said, *'Hey we're still here. We still care.'* And we haven't forgotten about you – even if your last payment was three weeks late.

✓ They knew what we were working on.

✓ They saw our latest projects.

And because of those little moments, those clients came back.

✓ They remembered us.

✓ They referred us.

✓ They trusted us.

✓ They came back to us instead of the competition.

So yeah—love letters work.

The thing is, marketing doesn't have to be loud. It just has to be real.

Sometimes it's a newsletter.

Sometimes it's a phone call or a follow-up email.

Sometimes, it's a coffee-stained handwritten note that says,

'Thanks for sticking with us. We see you.'

Do it well, **they recommend you. They defend you. They remember you.**

Even if your husband still forgets to send the invoice. They will wait for your availability.

They will send other people your way.

They become advocates because you made the effort to communicate.

And if you ask me, that's worth every teabag I've ever mailed.

(Just don't tell Andrew. He still thinks marketing's just putting up a sign on the Ute.)

Lessons Learned
Communication Isn't Just a Task—It's the Whole Damn Business Brand

...and possibly the reason you drink tea from a wine glass.

- ✓ Communication builds trust—and occasionally builds a wall between you and the client who wants to 'just pop over' on a Sunday.

- ✓ Marketing isn't just promotion—it's reputation repair, done with a smile and a spellcheck. Sometimes it's a glossy flyer, sometimes it's a coffee-stained note and a teabag stapled to a newsletter called a 'love letter.' Either way, they remember you.

- ✓ People return to people, not prices. You don't need to be the cheapest, flashiest, or even the

Documentation Matters

fastest. You just need to be *real*, responsive, and only slightly sarcastic.

- ✓ Loyalty doesn't come from discounts—it comes from connection. (And sometimes, knowing your client's dog's name better than your own kids' shoe sizes.)

- ✓ Boundaries don't break relationships—they build better ones. Saying *'Not today, mate'* is self-care, not sabotage.

- ✓ Write. Everything. Down. If it's not written, it never happened—according to every supplier who miraculously forgets what they promised five minutes after hanging up.

- ✓ Track every call, quote, and excuse—because one day, your phone log will win you a pricing argument and possibly a small battle in the war on supplier forgetfulness.

- ✓ Newsletters actually work. Even tradies who say they 'don't read emails' are apparently reading mine and calling them *'love letters.'* Cute… and effective.

- ✓ Admin isn't admin—it's operations, logistics, negotiation, and survival wrapped in one unpaid title. Especially when you're the only one who knows where the paperclip stash is and why we're still getting invoices for a job from last year.

- ✓ Yes, some men will assume you don't know what you're doing. Smile politely, take their money, fix their mistake, and send them a professionally formatted invoice... with a footnote that says, *'We told you so.'*

- ✓ Consistency = Credibility. Be the person who always follows up, always knows what's going on, and never loses their cool—unless the WiFi goes out during payroll.

Final Thought
Why Every Tradie Wife Deserves a Direct Line to a Lawyer, an Accountant, a Therapist and a Coach

After years of answering 6 am complaint calls, fighting with suppliers, and stopping clients from pulling fast ones, I have three must-haves for every woman running a business:

- ✓ A lawyer—because contracts mean nothing unless you enforce them.

- ✓ An accountant—because money is confusing, and tax is a nightmare.

- ✓ A therapist—because, well... see everything above.

- ✓ And a **coach or mentor** – to remind you that you are not losing your mind, you're just running a business with no job description and all the responsibility.

So yes, behind every great tradie is a woman rolling her eyes so hard she gives herself a migraine.

And if anyone dares to call me *'just the secretary'* one more time?

I'll happily hand them a phone, a bounced cheque, and a supplier dispute or customer who still owes us money, and say,

'Here, mate. If it's that easy, you have a go.'

Chapter 14

Balancing Babies, Business, and Board Meetings – Welcome to the Ultimate Juggle

Keeping the business running, the babies fed, and the building blocks from taking over the office.

The Business-Baby Balancing Act

Running a business while **raising a family** is a skill they **don't** teach in business school.

It's a mix of:

✓ Crisis management *(because someone always spills something at the worst time).*

✓ Negotiation skills *(because toddlers and suppliers both require strategic bargaining).*

✓ Event planning *(because balancing feeding times and toolbox meetings is an art).*

✓ Advanced stealth operations *(because answering a business call while hiding a noisy child is a mission).*

Now, if I had been running this operation **in today's world,** it might have been a little easier—wireless headsets, email communication, and the ability to step outside to take a call.

But no.

This was the **1990s.**

Which meant:

✗ No mobile phones *(unless you count Andrew's brick-sized truck phone, which was mostly for emergencies).*

✗   No work-from-home option.

✗   No Zoom meetings—if people needed to talk, they came to the office.

So, there I was, running an engineering business with a baby in one arm, a phone in the other, and a toddler or two sitting quietly nearby, trained to understand that *'Mummy's on the phone'* meant absolute silence... or at least a solid attempt at it.

Training Children Like Future CEOs (Or at least, future quiet humans in an office)

One of the first business lessons my children ever learned wasn't about money or management—it was about not interrupting Mum on the phone.

It took training. A lot of training.

At first, they'd scramble into my office mid-conversation, loudly declaring their latest crisis:

'Mum, he took my toy!'

'Mum, I'm hungry!'

'Mum, she's looking at me weird!'

But after many whispered warnings, firm reminders, and a few well-timed mummy-looks, they eventually learned the golden rule:

If something goes wrong, come sit on Mum's lap, have a cuddle, and wait. But DO. NOT. TALK. Until the phone goes down.

I'm not saying it was easy.

I'm saying it was necessary.

And after enough repetition, they got it.

If they had a bad moment, they'd wander over, climb onto my lap, and bury their little heads into my shoulder—silent, patient, waiting.

By the time I hung up, I'd pat their backs and say, 'Alright, what's the problem?'

Immediate explosion of words.

But hey, at least they had **waited**.

Breastfeeding in the Office – The Cloth Nappy Camouflage

Of course, feeding a baby in the **middle of a workday** was a whole other logistical challenge.

There were **no designated nursing rooms** or fancy breastfeeding-friendly setups.

There was just me, my baby, my desk, and a business to run.

So, I improvised.

- ✓ Portable cot in the corner? *Check.*
- ✓ A cloth nappy permanently draped over my shoulder as a quick cover-up? Absolutely.
- ✓ The ability to seamlessly go from 'business owner' to 'human milk bar' and back again? *Mastered.*

And honestly?

Most of the staff and clients didn't bat an eye.

At first, I worried about making them uncomfortable, but then I realised—if they didn't like it, they could look at the welding machine instead.

The funniest part?

Some staff and visitors were so awkward about it that they suddenly became very, very interested in the papers on my desk.

'Yep, just gonna stare at this invoice until it's safe to look up again.'

Bless them.

Meetings in the Office: The Best Receptionist in the World

Thankfully, I wasn't completely alone in this balancing act.

I had a fantastic receptionist who was the guardian of sanity.

- ✓ She knew which clients were fine with babies in the office and which ones weren't.
- ✓ She developed a sixth sense for when I needed backup.
- ✓ She became the official Baby Whisperer of the workplace.

If I was stuck on a long call and the baby got fussy, she'd swoop in and save the day.

If a client showed up and I was mid-feed, she'd casually stall them with coffee and small talk until I was ready.

Honestly?

I probably owe that woman **half my sanity** and at least one of my children's university funds.

Toolbox Meetings & Feeding Times – A Timing Disaster

Now, staff toolbox meetings and baby feeding schedules should have been completely unrelated.

And yet—without fail—they always clashed.

I'd be settling in for a quiet feeding session, hoping for a few calm, uninterrupted moments, when suddenly:

'Boss, toolbox meeting's starting!'

So what did I do?

- ✓ I threw the cloth nappy over my shoulder, adjusted the baby, and walked in like I meant business.
- ✓ I sat at the back, listening, nodding, and occasionally contributing, all while feeding my baby.
- ✓ I ignored the awkward glances from the younger tradies who clearly weren't sure where to look.

And honestly?

After a while, **they got used to it.**

Business is business—even when the boss is **feeding a baby at the same time.**

Lessons Learned
Running a Business with Babies in Tow

- ✓ Training your kids to stay quiet on the phone is possible—it just takes time (and cuddles).

- ✓ A cloth nappy over the shoulder is the ultimate breastfeeding business tool.

- ✓ A good receptionist is worth their weight in gold.

- ✓ Some clients and staff will awkwardly avoid eye contact while you breastfeed—let them.

- ✓ There's no perfect balance between babies and business—just a lot of creative problem-solving.

Final Thought
The Day I Stopped Apologising for Being a Mum at Work

For a long time, I worried that bringing my kids into the workplace would make me look **less professional.**

But I realised something—

Being a mother in business doesn't make you weaker. It makes you a master of efficiency, patience, and multitasking.

Because, behind every great tradie is a woman who can run a meeting, manage staff, negotiate contracts, and rock a baby to sleep—all in the same day.

And if anyone had a problem with that?

They could take it up with my quietly trained, phone-call-respecting, toolbox-meeting-surviving children.

Now, excuse me while I handle payroll with a toddler on my lap.

Chapter 15

Beyond the Toolbox – The Skills That Keep the Big Jobs Running

How I went from 'just helping out' to running the show (and keeping businesses from falling apart).

Big Jobs Need More Than Big Tools

Every business starts the same way—**a few jobs, a few blokes, and a whole lot of 'she'll be right' attitude.**

But then, suddenly, you're not just a **small operation** anymore.

✓   There's more work coming in than you can keep up with.

✓   The paperwork is piling up faster than you can shove it into a drawer.

✓   The team is growing, but no one's quite sure who's responsible for what.

✓   And somehow, even though you're busier than ever, **the cash flow is tighter than it should be.**

This is when a business can go one of two ways—**it either levels up and becomes a serious, well-run operation, or it drowns in its own chaos.**

That's when I learned the real difference between a business that **survives** and one that **thrives.**

And let me tell you—it's got nothing to do with **how good you are at your trade.**

It's about how well you **run the business behind the trade.**

The Bigger Picture – Seeing Beyond the Next Job

As we grew, I realised I wasn't just *'helping out'* by managing day-to-day tasks—I was creating the structure that allowed us to grow without falling apart.

✓ I wasn't just hiring staff—I was building a team and a workplace culture.

✓ I wasn't just keeping the finances in order—I was setting us up for financial stability.

✓ I wasn't just handling clients—I was developing long-term business relationships that brought repeat work.

✓ I wasn't just solving problems—I was creating systems that stopped the same problems from happening again.

And if there's one thing I know for sure, a business that only focuses on the next job will always be one step away from disaster.

Helen Cowley

Growing a Business? Here's What No One Tells You

Most tradies start small and grow fast—but no one prepares them for what happens when their business gets bigger than what they can personally control.

That's when everything starts getting messy.

✓ Jobs get delayed because materials weren't ordered in time.

✓ Clients get frustrated because no one's on top of scheduling.

✓ Payroll becomes a nightmare because there's no clear cash flow management.

✓ You find yourself stuck fixing the same mistakes over and over.

And suddenly, what used to feel like freedom now feels like a giant, stressful mess.

That's when the real skills come in—the ones **that separate the businesses that last from the ones that burn out.**

What I Learned (The hard way) About Running a Growing Business

Leadership Isn't Just About Giving Orders— It's About Creating a Team That Works Without You

- ✓ If you're the only one who knows what's going on, you're the problem.

- ✓ If your team relies on you to solve everything, you're the cause of the bottleneck.

- ✓ If your business falls apart when you take a holiday, you don't have a business—you have a very stressful job.

The biggest lesson I learned?

A **business needs structure**—clear roles, good communication, and people who know what they're doing without waiting for instructions.

Because if you have to personally manage every single thing—you're going to **burn out** before your business ever gets where it should be.

Cash Flow Is the Real Boss (And clients will try to take advantage of you)

Ah, *money*.

The one thing that **keeps a business alive**—and the one thing that so many tradies ignore until they're drowning in overdue invoices.

✓ Clients love delaying payments as long as possible.

✓ Banks don't care how many jobs you've got booked if your account is empty.

✓ And the tax office? *Well, they're never late sending their invoices.*

I learned that cash flow isn't about how much money you make—it's about how well you control it.

✓ If you don't track your numbers, you're flying blind.

✓ If you don't chase invoices, clients will push their luck.

✓ If you don't price properly, you'll work harder and earn less.

And if you don't **get a grip on your financials early**, you'll be **trading long hours for very little reward**.

Systems and Processes Are the Difference Between a Well-Oiled Machine and a Dumpster Fire

Ever had a job go **completely off track** because someone forgot to:

✓ Order the materials?

✓ Confirm the schedule?

✓ Tell the team what the plan actually was?

Yeah. Me too.

Turns out, businesses that *'figure it out as they go'* spend more time fixing mistakes than actually making money.

I started seeing the power of systems—things like:

✓ Having clear procedures for every job.

✓ Making sure everyone knows who's responsible for what.

✓ Setting up simple ways to track progress, timelines, and costs.

Because **guesswork is fine for fishing—not for running a business.**

Growth Without a Plan Is Just a Faster Road to Burnout

A lot of tradies think growing a business just means getting more work.

Wrong.

If you grow too fast without the right structure, you end up:

✓ Working twice as hard for half the profit.

✓ Overloading your team without the right support.

✓ Spending more time fixing problems than actually making progress.

The real key to growth?

✓ Know your numbers.

✓ Have a system for hiring and training.

✓ Build processes that keep things running smoothly.

Because **if you don't plan for growth, your business will outgrow you.**

Burnout Mindset – When the Business Owns You

At some point, when a business grows, you stop running it, and it starts running you.

For me, that moment came when I realised I was working harder than ever, but it no longer felt like my business—it felt like a weight I was carrying.

I was:

✓ Managing everything.

✓ Solving everyone's problems.

✓ Keeping everything afloat.

And at the end of the day?

There was **nothing left for me.**

The Signs You're in Burnout Mode

✓ You wake up and immediately feel overwhelmed.

✓ Every day feels like you're putting out fires.

✓ The business is doing well, but you don't feel good about it.

✓ You don't even know what you enjoy anymore.

✓ You have no time, **no energy, and no joy left** for yourself.

Burnout isn't just **physical exhaustion**—it's **emotional exhaustion.**

You start **losing yourself** in the process of keeping everyone else going.

And before you know it, **you're stuck in a business that no longer brings you joy**—just stress, pressure, and an endless to-do list.

The Moment I Realised I Was More Than the Business

One day, I caught myself saying *'I don't have time for that'*—about something I actually wanted to do.

And I stopped.

Because if I was **so busy working that I couldn't enjoy life anymore,** what was the point?

That was when I knew:

I needed to take back control—not just of the business, but of my life.

That meant:

✓ Setting boundaries.

✓ Building a team that didn't rely on me for every little thing.

✓ Remembering that I was more than just 'the person who makes everything run.'

And most importantly—**figuring out what I actually wanted.**

Because here's the truth:

A business should serve you—not the other way around.

And that leads me to the most important chapter of all…

Leading Into 'Wait… What About Me?'

For years, I was **everything to everyone**—the one who had all the answers, the one who could fix every problem, the one who made sure everything ran smoothly.

But somewhere along the way, **I lost sight of myself.**

It's easy to do when you're constantly busy, constantly solving, constantly giving.

But one day, you look up and realise:

'Wait... what about me?'

✓ What do I actually want?

✓ What makes me happy outside of work?

✓ Who am I when I'm not fixing, managing, or organising?

And the truth is—if you don't stop to ask yourself those questions, you'll wake up one day feeling lost.

It's time to **reclaim yourself.**

Because behind every great business is a person who deserves to live, thrive, and find joy—not just work themselves into the ground.

Lessons Learned
What Every Growing Business Needs

If your business is getting **bigger, busier, and harder to control,** here's what I know for sure:

✓ If you don't have a plan, your business will run you instead of the other way around.

✓ If your cash flow is messy, it'll choke your growth before you even realise what's happening.

✓ If you don't create systems, you'll spend half your life fixing the same problems.

✓ If your team isn't structured properly, everything will end up on your plate.

And most importantly:

A successful business isn't built on hard work alone—it's built on strategy, structure, and smart decisions.

Final Thought
A Business That Grows Shouldn't Shrink You

Success isn't just about building a great business—**it's about building a great life.**

Yes If I've learned anything from building, managing, and growing a business, it's this:

✓ Good tradespeople don't always make good business owners—until they learn how to run the business side properly.

✓ Systems, leadership, and financial control aren't just 'extras'—*they're what keep a business alive.*

✓ Success isn't about getting bigger—it's about getting better.

Because behind every great business isn't just hard work and long hours—it's a plan that makes all that effort actually pay off.

And if you want a business that runs smoothly, grows properly, and doesn't drive you to an early retirement (or mental breakdown), it's time to think bigger than just the next job.

But:

Because behind every great tradie, behind every successful business, behind every long list of achievements, is a person who deserves to feel fulfilled, not just exhausted.

And if you're reading this thinking, *'I've been so caught up in running things that I've forgotten what I actually want',* then it's **time to change that.**

Because the **most important thing you'll ever build... is yourself.**

Now, let's talk about **taking back your joy.**

Chapter 16

'Wait, What About Me?' – Reclaiming Your Life & Sanity

How I stopped being just 'the woman behind the man' and became my own person.

The Moment I Realised I Had Lost Myself

For years, I poured **everything** into Andrew's business.

- ✓ I learned HR, finance, marketing, and project management.
- ✓ I built systems, trained staff, and handled clients.
- ✓ I raised five kids. *(Yes, five. While also running a business.)*
- ✓ I became the fixer of every single problem.

And somewhere in all of that...

I lost myself. Lost who I thought I was – the fashion designer, dressmaker, homemaker, creative artist, the gardener, the person who was about family. I was the daughter, the mother, the sister. Who had no skills, no qualifications, and I was lost.

It wasn't **one big moment.**

It was the **thousands of small moments** where I put **everyone else first**—Andrew, the kids, the staff, the clients. Who was I?

Until one day, I sat down and thought:

'If I'm so bloody good at running a business... why the hell am I not running my own?'

When Clients Saw My Value Before I Did

Ironically, while I was **doubting myself,** some of our **clients weren't.**

More than once, a business owner would pull me aside and say:

'You're really good at this stuff. Have you ever thought about doing this for other businesses, or for our business?'

And my immediate response?

'Oh, no... I'm just helping out.'

Helping out?!

I had **built an entire business infrastructure** from the ground up, **developed systems and processes,** and kept everything **running smoothly while raising a family.**

And yet, I didn't think **I was qualified.**

Why?

Because I didn't have a **degree, a title, or any official recognition.** Because I was a woman in a man's industry?

And also, because I was so **wrapped up in Andrew's dream** that I had forgotten to ask:

'Wait, what about me?'

The Two Big Lies I Told Myself

Looking back, there were two major lies I believed that kept me stuck for far too long:

Lie Number 1: I'm Not Qualified

I thought that because I didn't have a **fancy degree**, I couldn't possibly be a business consultant or expert in anything.

Reality check:

- ✓ I had real-world experience running and growing a successful company.
- ✓ I had more hands-on knowledge than half the 'qualified' consultants out there.
- ✓ I had proven results.

A piece of paper wouldn't have made me **any better at solving business problems.**

I was already doing the work—**I just hadn't given myself permission to own it.**

Lie Number 2: Who Am I to Do This?

Imposter syndrome is a **sneaky little bastard**.

It whispers things like:

'You're not an expert—you're just good at organising things.'

'You just got lucky.'

'Nobody will take you seriously.'

'You're just doing the admin' or simply

'You're a woman'

Meanwhile, **real business owners** were asking for my help because they could see my **value**—even when I couldn't.

Reaching My Breaking Point: The Moment I Chose Myself

After wrapping up yet another exhausting contract, I was done. Completely, utterly spent.

- ✓ I didn't want to talk about staff issues.
- ✓ I didn't want to hear about contract negotiations.
- ✓ I didn't even want to think about what came next.

I just wanted to go home, curl up, and breathe.

Our lease was up for renewal, and I was up for a renew too.

Between the business, the kids, and the never-ending stress, I had lost my way. I needed a break—**and then, I needed something for myself.** But what?

That question lingered until eventually I found my own way and own strategies for getting out of the overdone 'below the line' attitude I had created in myself.

'I'm taking on my own clients. I'm setting my own boundaries. And I'm running things on my terms.'

And do you know what he said?

'Yeah, Hon. That makes sense.'

...That's it?!

After years of putting everything else first, sacrificing my own ambitions, waiting for the *right time*—he just assumed I'd do my own thing when I was ready.

That's when it hit me: the only person who lost themselves in someone else and who had been holding me back... **was me.**

The Art of Letting Go: Downsizing a Business the Hard Way

Deciding to **downsize a business** isn't just about shutting the doors and calling it a day. It's not as simple as handing in your lease and walking away, especially when you've built something brick by brick. It's **messy, emotional, and full of unexpected roadblocks**—a bit like cleaning out a house after years of hoarding, except instead of old junk, you're dealing with **contracts, suppliers, staff, and entire shipping containers full of equipment.**

We had made the decision: **no more premises, less staff, no more tendering.** It was time to strip things back, get lean, and focus on what Andrew really loved working on—**the mobile service that didn't come with as many headaches for me to maintain.**

But, of course, getting from *decision to done* was a battle in itself.

Step 1: Breaking Up with the Lease (And the Mess It Left Behind)

You don't truly realise how much stuff you've accumulated until you have to **pack it all up and move it.** And within a limited time. What started as a 'simple clean-out' turned into a **full-scale extraction mission.**

✓ Negotiating the lease exit – *because landlords don't just wave goodbye with a smile.*

✓ Sorting through years of paperwork, spare parts, and *'we might need this one day'* junk.

✓ Figuring out where to stash Andrew's beloved, oversized relics—*because apparently, 'It's still got life in it!' is a valid argument when discussing a two-tonne piece of machinery from the Jurassic era. So, instead of offloading it, we had to relocate the beasts like they were part of a witness protection program.*

And, of course, there was the emotional part—closing the doors on a place that had been the heart of the business for years. But sentimentality doesn't pay the bills when it is time to move on.

Step 2: Unwinding Supplier Agreements (Without Burning Bridges)

Suppliers love you when you're placing big orders. When you tell them you're downsizing? Not so much.

✓ Negotiating out-of-supply contracts without paying through the nose.

✓ Explaining that, no, I won't be needing bulk deliveries anymore (and no, I don't need a 'special deal' to stay).

✓ Making sure we could still get materials on a smaller scale when needed at a reasonable price.

Step 3: Saying Goodbye to Staff (And Managing the Fallout)

Letting go of staff is never easy. Some took it well, some... not so much.

✓ Honest conversations about why we were shutting down the full operation.

✓ Making sure everyone was paid out properly *(because burning bridges in a small industry isn't a good strategy)*.

✓ Dealing with the guilt of knowing this decision affected more than just me.

Some moved on quickly, others needed time to process it. But at the end of the day, a business has to work for you, not the other way around. And I was done.

Step 4: The Logistics Nightmare – Moving Heavy Equipment

There's nothing quite like realising you have literal container loads of equipment that need to be relocated, sold, or scrapped.

✓ Finding storage for what we still needed.

✓ Selling off what we didn't.

✓ Moving it all without breaking the bank (or my back).

It was **chaos,** but piece by piece, we made it happen.

Step 5: Same Business, Less Baggage

Once the dust settled (and the last shipping container was finally closed), we weren't *reinventing the business*—we were just ditching the dead weight and focusing on what actually worked. No grand rebranding, no flashy relaunch—just doing what we'd always done, but without the headache of a physical premises.

✓ No more rent, no more overheads, no more wondering why the electricity bill was higher than a five-star resort.

✓ No more staff dramas—just us, the tools, and the open road (minus the occasional flat tyre).

✓ More control, less chaos, and (finally) the ability to ignore calls at 5 am guilt-free.

Downsizing wasn't easy. It wasn't quick. But in the end, it was the best decision we could have made. Because business isn't always about scaling up—it's about knowing when you have had enough, knowing when to strip it back, cut the nonsense, and run it in a way that makes sense – *'working to live not living to work'.*

—it's about **knowing when to pivot, when to let go, and when to start fresh and reinventing yourself**

Lessons Learned
How to Build Your Own Identity While Supporting Others

✓ Helping your husband build his dream is great, but don't lose your own in the process.

✓ You don't need a degree to be an expert—experience is just as valuable.

✓ If clients see your value before you do, LISTEN TO THEM.

✓ Imposter syndrome is a liar—don't let it keep you stuck.

✓ Boundaries aren't just nice to have—they're necessary.

✓ If you find yourself in a hole, below the line, maybe read my 'Helen Cowley Business Mastery Journal' or 'Overcome with gratitude' stories

Final Thought
Owning My Own Success

It took years of trial, error, and sheer stubbornness, and a bit of a breakdown, but I finally understood something I wish I had realised sooner:

I wasn't just *helping out.*

I wasn't just the *woman behind the business.*

I was the business.

And not just the nuts and bolts—I was **HR, marketing, finance, business planning, and everything in between.** Oh, and welding—knowing good from bad. Because apparently, that was part of the job description too.

And now, when someone dares to ask, *'Who are you to be a business consultant?'* I just smile and say:

'I'm the woman who built an empire while raising five kids. Who the hell are you?'

Because behind every great tradie isn't just a woman rolling her eyes... she's the one keeping the whole damn operation running and building her own legacy while she's at it.

Here's to you—building businesses, raising families, and proving every damn day that you are more than just 'helping out.'

Afterword

A Woman, A Business, and a Life Worth Living

If you've made it this far, congratulations—you've survived the rollercoaster ride of business, tradies, chaos, and the occasional moment of absolute genius.

You've read about late-night business plans, clients who think Christmas morning is a great time for a service call, the endless juggling of work and family, and the quiet, unnoticed skills that keep businesses (and households) running smoothly.

And if there's one thing I hope you take from this book, it's this:

You are more capable, more skilled, and more important than you probably give yourself credit for.

Whether you're **running a business, supporting one, or thinking about stepping into your own,** the truth is—you've probably been doing it **all along,** without ever recognising it.

For the Tradie Who Wants to Grow (and keep his sanity in the process)

If you're a tradie running a growing business, this book wasn't just about having a laugh at the chaos—it was also about showing you the bigger picture.

✓ Success isn't just about working harder—it's about working smarter.

✓ Your business will only grow as well as the systems and leadership behind it.

✓ You don't have to do it all alone—your best asset might be right beside you.

Many tradies build businesses without thinking about the long-term plan—until one day, the business is bigger than they can personally control.

That's when you **start drowning in the work instead of running it.**

If you want to **grow without burning out,** here's what I've learned:

✓ Get your finances in order—cash flow is king.

✓ Create systems that make the business work without you doing everything.

✓ Hire good people—and let them take responsibility.

✓ Hire the coach or consultant before the breakdown, not after. Trust me, it's cheaper than therapy and far more tax-deductible.

✓ And most importantly—recognise the skills and support of the person beside you.

If your partner is already helping out, running the admin, handling customers, managing the books, keeping things afloat while you're on-site—**she's not just 'helping'**—she's already a business leader.

Treat her as your business partner. Include her in decisions. Respect the skills she brings.

Because if you work together as a team, **you're not just running a business—you're building something bigger than both of you.**

The Lessons I Didn't Know I was Learning

Looking back, I can see now that every part of my journey—from managing invoices to managing staff, from juggling babies to juggling contracts, from *'just helping out'* to **leading a business**—was teaching me something.

✓   How to be a leader *(even when I didn't feel like one)*.

✓   How to set boundaries *(even when it felt easier to say yes)*.

✓   How to keep the business running *(without losing myself in the process)*.

✓   How to develop focused strategies that drive real growth *(without drowning in unnecessary tasks.)*

- ✓ How your mindset isn't just about pushing through—it's about shifting how you see the business, your role, and your future.

Because your mindset will make the difference between you wanting to quit, or create something bigger.

A business doesn't just grow by **working harder**—it grows by **working smarter**

And most importantly—**how to build something that worked for me, not just something I worked for.**

If You're Feeling Stuck, Read This

If you're feeling like you've lost yourself somewhere in the business, in the day-to-day grind, in the **constant cycle of 'just getting through'**—take a step back.

Because I promise you, **it's not too late** to reclaim yourself.

- ✓ You are more than the business.
- ✓ You are more than the daily demands.
- ✓ You are not just 'the person who keeps everything running.'

You deserve to find **joy, to build something you love, and to feel like YOU again.**

So, What's Next?

That's the best part—**whatever you want it to be.**

✓ Maybe it's growing the business—but doing it in a way that actually gives you freedom.

✓ Maybe it's stepping into leadership—owning the skills you've had all along.

✓ Maybe it's finally **putting yourself first**—after years of putting everyone else ahead of you.

Whatever it is, **know this:**

You've got this.

You've **always had this.**

It's just time to start believing it.

Final Thought: Behind Every Great Business is a Woman Who Knows Her Worth.

You are not just *'helping out.'* You are not just *'doing admin.'* You are not just *'supporting.'*

You are a leader, a strategist, a problem-solver, a business builder, and a force to be reckoned with.

And whether you choose to build an empire or simply build a life that makes you happy, know that you have the skills, the knowledge, and the power to do it.

Now go out there and **make the business—and the life—that YOU want.**

Because behind every great tradie, there's a woman rolling her eyes... but also keeping the whole damn thing running.

Thank you for reading, for laughing along the way, and for recognising just how powerful you really are.

Now, go claim your next chapter—whatever that looks like for you.

www.ingramcontent.com/pod-product-compliance
Lightning Source LLC
Chambersburg PA
CBHW020531080526
44583CB00013B/813